Last
Letters of
Resistance

Last Letters of Resistance

Farewells from the Bonhoeffer Family

Edited by Eberhard & Renate Bethge

Translated by Dennis Slabaugh

FORTRESS PRESS   PHILADELPHIA

Translated by Dennis Slabaugh

Translation of *Letzte Briefe im Widerstand: Aus dem Kreis der Familie Bonhoeffer* copyright © 1984 by Chr. Kaiser Verlag, Munich, West Germany.

Cover photograph by Eberhard Röhm is used by permission of Chr. Kaiser Verlag.

Scripture quotations are from the Holy Bible, King James Version.

The letter on pp. 36–37 has been translated from the French by Gary Phillips.

The poems "Stations on the Road to Freedom," "Powers of Good," and "Jonah" from Dietrich Bonhoeffer, *Letters and Papers from Prison*, The Enlarged Edition, Copyright © 1971 by SCM Press, pp. 370–71, 398–99, 400–401, are used by permission of the publishers, SCM Press and Macmillan Publishing Company.

Library of Congress Cataloging-in-Publication Data

Letzte Briefe im Widerstand. English.

Last letters of resistance.

Translation of: Letzte Briefe im Widerstand.
1. Anti-Nazi movement—Germany. 2. World War,
1939–1945—Underground movements—Germany. 3. Germany—
Politics and government—1933–1945. 4. Bonhoeffer
family—Correspondence. 5. Political prisoners—
Germany—Correspondence. 6. Hitler, Adolf, 1889–1945—
Assassination attempt, 1944 (July 20) I. Bethge,
Eberhard, 1909–   . II. Bethge, Renate. III. Title.
DD256.3.L4713 1986   943.086'092'4   85–45504
ISBN 0–8006–1884–X

1811K85   Printed in the United States of America   1–1884

With many victims of the final weeks of the war, 1945, here rest

Klaus Bonhoeffer	Hans John	Hans Ludwig Sierks
5 January 1901	31 August 1911	24 July 1877
Carl Adolf Marks	Wilhelm zur Nieden	Richard Klenzer
14 February 1894	29 August 1878	6 September 1875
Friedrich Justus Perels		Rüdiger Schleicher
3 November 1910		14 January 1895

Died in the night of 22–23 April 1945 near their prison at Lehrterstrasse

Like these, the following suffered death in the
resistance of injustice and violence.

Dietrich Bonhoeffer	Justus Delbrück	Hans von Dohnanyi
4 February 1906–	25 November 1902–	1 January 1902–
9 April 1945	21 October 1945	April 1945
in Flossenbürg		in Sachsenhausen
Concentration Camp		Concentration Camp

Blessed are those who are persecuted for righteousness' sake,
for theirs is the kingdom of heaven

CONTENTS

INTRODUCTION

1

This collection of testimonies by members of the Bonhoeffer family from the period before they were killed in connection with the plot of 20 July 1944 contains more than genuine farewell letters. Strictly speaking, only Klaus Bonhoeffer's letters from the Lehrter Street prison of April 1945 are clear farewell letters resembling a legacy. Rüdiger Schleicher, in the same prison, wrote one like it for his family. He had this letter with him during one of the last visits from his wife, Ursula, in the Lehrter Street prison, but he kept it back so as, if possible, not to worry her unnecessarily, as he said. Neither wanted to give up the struggle for survival yet, even if both were prepared for every possibility. The will not to give up in the chaos of early 1945 seems also to have governed Hans von Dohnanyi and Dietrich Bonhoeffer too much for them to write an indication of farewell. If, however, something of the kind was written by them too, it has in any case been destroyed. To be sure, Dietrich Bonhoeffer several times after the failure of 20 July expressed himself as in a legacy, and these literary testimonies are printed here. Should something similar be found in his letters to his fiancée, Maria von Wedemeyer, that still remains inaccessible because before her death in 1977 she extended once again the exclusionary clause for her correspondence with Dietrich Bonhoeffer for another twenty-five years. The diary entries of Justus Delbrück, Klaus Bonhoeffer's brother-in-law and fellow prisoner at Lehrter Street, and his letter to his son show clearly the characteristics of a deliberate legacy, yet are not a farewell letter.

2

The impetus for the publication of this collection was a recent examination of old letters. Along with the long-known last testimonies from Hans von Dohnanyi, Justus Delbrück, and Dietrich and Klaus Bonhoeffer, there were also many testimonies from Rüdiger Schleicher's last days. They show even more completely the composure with which the Bonhoeffer family endured the end that befell them almost without parallel after the failure of 20 July 1944. No shadow fell upon the common dedication of this family during the hardest test; they each knew that the heart of the other reacted as their own, whether in the cells or in the house of the parents or in the exile of the Leibholz siblings at Oxford. The worldwide interest in the spirit and role of this family in the German resistance against National Socialism is an encouragement to the publication of these "last letters." Willem Visser't Hooft wrote in 1945, in an obituary of Dietrich Bonhoeffer, "The nihilists of the Third Reich encountered in the Bonhoeffer house a center of a high-minded spirit from the best German tradition, a spirit which neither could, nor wanted to, come to terms with their inhumanity" (*Das Zeugnis eines Boten* [The witness of a messenger] [Geneva, 1945], 4).

3

For the selection of the present testimonies, it was necessary to establish certain dates. Such dates do not coincide easily for the five witnesses. For Rüdiger Schleicher, just as for Klaus Bonhoeffer, a crucial day is 2 February 1945, on which the president of the People's

Tribunal,[1] Roland Freisler, announced their death sentences, after which "last letters" had to be expected. However, it proved appropriate to accept, too, earlier letters from Rüdiger Schleicher to his wife from prison, as well as two letters from Klaus Bonhoeffer to his sons from the year before. They are in startling contrast to the tremendous suspense in which he found himself during the assassination attempt on 20 July 1944; they are so much occupied with his children that they betray hardly anything at all of what the last phase demanded of him. For Hans von Dohnanyi, after all the preceding changes that produced ever more alarming situations, the new, last, and serious one emerges with his transfer from the infirmary of the concentration camp at Sachsenhausen to the basement cells of Prinz-Albrecht Street, the so-called home prison of the Reich Central Security Office,[2] in the first days of February 1945. There, by the way, his brother-in-law Dietrich Bonhoeffer spoke with him once again shortly; he had succeeded during an air raid in slipping unseen into Hans von Dohnanyi's infirmary cell. For Dietrich Bonhoeffer, it was important to select from the well-known publications—above all from *Widerstand und Ergebung*,[3] what he himself wrote down in a letter or literary text as a kind of summa before the ever-expected end. Thus we selected the letter written immediately after receiving news of the failed *Putsch;* farewells like "Stations of the Way to Freedom" or, somewhat later, "Jonah"; but then too, the two actual last letters we possess, in which the language (concerned more with a collection of clothing than with the last farewell) is so profanely and tactically attuned to the attentive gaze of the SS censor. Justus Delbrück, who apparently had not been placed on the murder list by

1. [The *Volksgerichtshof* was established in 1934 as a special court to deal with cases of treason and high treason as well as other political crimes. It was used to suppress dissent to National Socialist rule and, in particular, against members of the resistance. There was no appealing the decisions of this court, which often required the death penalty. (Notes in brackets are by the translator.)]

2. [The *Reichssicherheitshauptamt* was established in 1939 as the chief security apparatus in the Reich. It included the Gestapo, formed an important part of the SS machine, and was led (until 1942) by the notorious Reinhard Heydrich.]

3. [The 2d ed. of this work is used here: *Widerstand und Ergebung: Briefe und Aufzeichnungen aus der Haft*, ed. Eberhard Bethge (Munich: Christian Kaiser Verlag, 1977). Material from the 1st ed. (Munich, 1970) was translated and published as Dietrich Bonhoeffer, *Letters and Papers from Prison: The Enlarged Edition*, ed. Eberhard Bethge (New York: Macmillan Co., 1971).]

the Gestapo, used the loneliness of his cell for days and weeks to leave behind, before an expected end, an account of his life and a legacy for his family.

4

Dietrich Bonhoeffer's reference to the NS clothing collection already indicates important differences in the character of these last testimonies to which we must be attentive. The reader is pulled to and fro, from the reading of smuggled secret messages to that of officially approved and censored letters. One reads sentences, indeed whole paragraphs, whose wording is indebted to the consideration taken of the reader in the Reich Central Security Office or even at the post office, like, for example, the ominous Commissar Sonderegger or the police guard of Lehrter Street and, in many cases, finally, the *Wehrmacht*[4] postal service. These wordings, in spite of the consideration taken of the other reader, also always include something authentic between the lines. An impressive example, among others, of this is the letter, included here, from Ursula Schleicher to her son in the field, in which she must inform him of the death sentence given his father. Where it is possible, therefore, the circumstances of the letter and the path taken by it are indicated in each case before the text.

5

Preceding each group of letters is a sketch about the writer. In most cases, relatives tell about their father, their husband, their brother. In some cases, hitherto unpublished writings that had been composed by relatives soon after 1945 for Ricarda Huch recommended themselves. These certainly do not report everything we would like to know, but they are very close to the emotions of those months. Ricarda Huch had asked for help for a book about the victims of 20 July in which she also wanted to report on Klaus and Dietrich Bon-

---

4. [From 1935 to 1945, the several military services in Germany carried the collective name of *Wehrmacht*, which can be translated only inadequately as "armed forces."]

hoeffer, on Hans von Dohnanyi and Rüdiger Schleicher (at that time, one could still have hopes for Justus Delbrück's survival). During the preparations for this book, however, she was overtaken by death. Thus the biographical sketches for the respective groups of letters show a varied character and even possess a varying informative value. One ought not take exception to this.

6

This volume does not intend to offer a complete history of these five persons. In the case of Dietrich Bonhoeffer, that already has been widely—and controversially—attempted elsewhere and is not to be repeated here. Something similar will occur for Hans von Dohnanyi in the next few years if comprehensive research projects already under way finally reach their goal. In these projects, of course, more light will fall also on the picture of the lives of Klaus Bonhoeffer, Rüdiger Schleicher, and Justus Delbrück. This means, however, that this book is not quite a critical presentation and assessment of their political profiles, of their posthumous writings, or of their special professional or historical achievements. Thus one also cannot expect from this volume any critical assessment of their respective parts in the conspiratorial activities in the National Socialist period; that must be carried out elsewhere. And this, too, will bring its own problems. It is likely to become apparent that some things, indeed many, are hardly to be reconstructed. Almost none of the witnesses of those events are any longer alive, and important documents are lacking. The published "Kaltenbrunner Reports," made to Hitler about the interrogations after 20 July—also, the interrogations of these five— are not "protocols" but rather merely records drawn up by the interrogating side, of the ominous, extreme quandary in which the prisoners found themselves. They hold, therefore, doubtful value as a source.

7

Yet, perhaps the documents in this volume prepare the ground for such work, since they convey something of the spirit of resistance that sustained the victims and their surviving relatives. This is served by the addition of the two items concerning the "Thereafter" in the Bonhoeffer family, including the account from the brother Karl-Friedrich, who survived, and the brief communication from the father to a former assistant.

8

None of the five men who are here personally documented would have wanted to be set apart from the other authors and victims of the conspiracy of 20 July 1944. There are still many other testimonies from the circle of conspirators that are at least as moving. The selection of these five was undertaken by us, and while completing it, we are already beset with the feeling that we are setting questionable limits. Under the aspect of the broader family circle, a number of others could have been included. One of these is General Paul von Hase, commandant of Berlin, executed as early as 8 August 1944: he was a cousin of the mother, Paula Bonhoeffer. Another is Ernst von Harnack, a cousin of the Delbrück siblings, who was dragged from the Lehrter Street Prison to his execution on 3 March 1945. There is also Peter Graf Yorck von Wartenburg, who was, after all, related by marriage. There are last letters from these three in the volume of collected writings edited by Helmut Gollwitzer, Käthe Kuhn, and Reinhold Schneider, *Du hast mich heimgesucht bei Nacht: Abschiedsbriefe und Aufzeichnungen des Widerstandes 1933–45* [You ravaged me in the night: Farewell letters and papers of the resistance 1933–45] (Munich, 1954). See there, for example, letters from Ernst von Harnack, on pp. 258–62, and from Peter Graf Yorck, on pp. 217–18, and on pp. 151–52 testimonies from Justus Delbrück, with a moving message of farewell to his wife. The editors intended their collection of farewell letters at that time to be "not only a reverently preserved memorial, an admonition and warning, but the bread of life we cannot do without in the reconstruction of our injured health" (p. 7). The intention of this small volume is no different.

Eberhard and Renate Bethge

RÜDIGER SCHLEICHER

Born 14 January 1895 in Stuttgart—in August 1914, as a soldier, severely wounded—1919, entrance into the civil service in Württemberg after legal studies—1922, called to Berlin as assessor in the Reich Ministry of Transportation—1923, marriage to Ursula Bonhoeffer—1924, doctoral dissertation on "Das internationale Luftfahrtrecht" [International aviation law]—work on the commentary on the air traffic law—after transfer into the Reich Aviation Ministry, director of the legal department there, with the rank of ministerial counselor until 1939, then associate professor and director of the Institute for the Law of the Air at Berlin University—arrested 3 October 1944—condemned to death 2 February 1945 by the People's Tribunal—shot 23 April.

Reminiscence

When the National Socialists seized power in Germany on 30 January 1933, my father commented on this event with the words, "This means war!" I was nine years old then, and I still remember clearly an ensuing vehement exchange of words with a different-minded distant relative that ended with the result that we did not—as I had hoped—watch together the spectacular torchlight parade with which

7

Hitler's followers celebrated this day. For Rüdiger Schleicher there existed from the beginning no doubt at all about the unscrupulousness and danger of the National Socialist "movement," and therefore, he had to reject totally the new regime. This attitude, which was immediately justified by events, was for him a matter of conscience and of justice; it led him finally into the resistance for which he paid with his death.

Rüdiger Schleicher was born on 14 January 1895 in Stuttgart. His paternal and maternal families were for a long time resident in Württemberg; his two grandfathers were jurists and highly competent senior administrative officers in the Württemberg civil service. His father was a much-respected and -loved Stuttgart doctor; he appears to have been of a rather serious nature. The artistic element in Rüdiger's personality certainly came more from his mother, Gertrud Rüdinger Schleicher. She is described as a very charming and educated woman who, along with the responsibility for a large, very convivial family, still found time for volunteer tasks—for example, with the Red Cross—and for handicrafts and literary work.

Rüdiger was the oldest of four brothers. In 1913, he completed his *Abitur*[1] and—after a short stay in England—had nearly ended his military service when the First World War broke out. As early as August 1914, he was severely wounded, and far into the last years of his life he had to suffer again and again from severe attacks of fever as a result of this wound.

From 1915 to 1919, Rüdiger Schleicher studied law in Tübingen. He became a member of the Hedgehogs, a fraternity without colors and dueling, in which many sons of Swabian "notables" had come together and to which his father and future father-in-law had also belonged. Although its members were generally fellow countrymen, an animated cosmopolitan atmosphere nevertheless ruled there, in which Rüdiger Schleicher gained friendships that continued to the end of his life. His violin playing made him a popular guest at student parties and on boat trips—his "student digs" lay on the Neckar right

---

1. [The *Abitur* is a comprehensive examination completed by students before entrance into university study.]

next to the tower in which Hölderlin had spent some of the last years of his life.

In the period after the end of the war, Rüdiger Schleicher was temporarily a member of the German Democratic Party,[2] influenced certainly above all by the writings of Friedrich Naumann, which had filled the young man with enthusiasm for a democratic liberalism on the basis of Christian and social responsibility. He preserved this basic political outlook for the rest of his life, referring readily to Naumann after the time of his party membership.

After his studies, Rüdiger Schleicher first of all entered the civil service in Württemberg, and from there he was sent on a leave of absence, from 1922 to 1925, to Berlin to the Reich Aviation Ministry of Transportation as a legal assessor. Here he was entrusted with questions concerning the law of the air, to which his dissertation too was devoted.

The atmosphere of Berlin, which in many respects stood in contrast to a certain sedateness and narrowness in his own hometown, so fascinated him from the beginning that after an intervening stay with the Chief Administrative Office of his home city of Stuttgart, he returned to Berlin. In spite of this, he remained a Swabian at heart who never completely lost a certain homesickness for Württemberg and his Swabian dialect.

In the period of his first stay in Berlin his marriage to Ursula Bonhoeffer occurred. This, along with the foundation of his own family, opened up for him a new circle of people that was to acquire decisive significance for his later life.

His professional career in Berlin led him from the rank of government counselor in the Aviation Department of the Reich Transportation Ministry to that of ministerial counselor and—until 1939— director of the legal department in the Reich Aviation Ministry. Here he was occupied primarily with administrative tasks and legislative activity. In 1939, he was named an associate lecturer for air law, and in 1940, he was entrusted with the directorship of the Institute of the

2. [The present-day Free Democratic Party in West Germany is successor to the prewar German Democratic Party and accepts Friedrich Naumann as one of its spiritual fathers.]

Law of the Air, relocated from Leipzig to the University of Berlin. He valued very highly this scientific and instructional work, which provided a balance to the more and more unpleasant service in the Ministry, and he devoted himself to it with special love. This found expression in a series of articles in professional journals, in the editing of the *Archiv für Luftrecht* [Archive for the law of the air], and above all, in a commentary on the law of the air, which, published repeatedly and reissued after the war, became a standard work in its field.

Rüdiger Schleicher was a jurist and civil servant of great dedication and a high sense of responsibility. He wanted to serve his state and not private interests. Therefore, he always refused to leave the civil service—even after 1933 and although he had received a tempting offer from private business.

A civil servant with such a conception of the state and duty had to encounter severe conflicts when the dictatorship took hold. In the reestablished Reich Aviation Ministry, in which he had been retained, the pressure to join the NSDAP was especially strong. With a heavy heart, he decided, for the sake of remaining in office, to make the additional sacrifice of joining the party. He hoped through this step to preserve possibilities of influence with which he could work against a total usurpation of public life by the new ruler. I still remember how on the evening of the last possible day before the deadline for registration in the party in May 1933, my father paced back and forth with me in front of the door of the party office until the office closed and he had to knock in order to be able to declare his entry into the party. Within the family, this entrance was discussed for a long time, especially in view of the family's opportunity to maintain, through Rüdiger Schleicher's remaining in office, important vantage points and contacts.

The membership in the party was judged at the death sentence an especially aggravating circumstance. Nevertheless, my father said even afterwards that he stood by the step from that time because it had enabled him to help many who were in distress—which in his eyes obviously carried more weight than the blemish he had thereby taken upon himself.

In the civil service, Rüdiger Schleicher saw the opportunity, appropriate to him, to serve the law. His relationship to the law, his service to the law, had an almost religious character for him. He was a conscious, yet liberal, Christian who did not take the easy way out when it came to his faith. The words "Your kingdom come" and "Seek first the kingdom of God and his righteousness, and all these things shall be added to you" were of primary significance for him. He saw his own striving for justice and truth entirely in this sense.

The effort always to do justice to his fellow human beings was revealed in all his behavior. It, in unison with the gift of being able to listen, and with a fundamentally cheerful, indeed often radiant, nature, opened to him the hearts of almost all who came into closer contact with him. Distrust of his fellow human beings lay far from his nature, and even when there could be no doubt anymore about the evil intentions of another, he still tried to understand the person. He did not want to become a judge in criminal cases, and in 1939 he refused a promotion that would have led him to this. With his great— at times almost overly scrupulous—conscientiousness, he would not have been able to tolerate in the long run the doubts about whether he had judged a defendant really justly, especially in a more and more strongly politicized justice system. His sincerity and goodness were at times disarming. With them, he won over even his prison guards, so that one of them ran after his lawyer and implored him to do everything he possibly could to save him.

Music had quite a special significance for my father. For him, it was, as a friend once said, "a window through which he could see into another world"; he himself would have considered even the word "revelation" appropriate in certain cases. He possessed a perfect ear, played the violin well, and loved above all to play chamber music with the family or with good friends. Opportunities to sing together, often on Sunday around the piano, where Father, freely harmonizing, accompanied chorales, and later, trios and quartets, were not least of all moments of relaxation in the increasingly difficult and burdensome years. In confinement his love for music was to prove itself a strong, sustaining force.

One does justice to the personality of Rüdiger Schleicher only when his family is included in the context. And "family" here was not only his own, with wife and four children; rather, it encompassed—after the early death of his own parents—the parents and siblings of his wife too.

His own family was in equal measure a responsibility and a source of strength for my father. We children were reared in the bourgeois Christian tradition, and our parents made no secret of their attitude toward National Socialism. The trust relationship was so strong that even toward the still very small children, they were astonishingly open with political information and declarations, which they dared to offer in the interest of a responsible education.

Because the Bonhoeffer parents lived from 1935 in the neighboring house, there existed an especially close contact with them and their children. That was especially true for the Dohnanyis, who likewise for a while lived close by, for Klaus Bonhoeffer and his family, and above all, from about 1940, for Dietrich, who from then on lived and worked most of the time in his parents' house and was also a sought-after pianist for at-home music making. The Bonhoeffer family circle was, in its diversity and at the same time in its internal unanimity, certainly unparalleled. All academic faculties were represented here and decidedly artistic talents were also not lacking. If there may have been slightly different shades of political opinion, there existed no doubt at all about a common basic democratic attitude; the Nazis quite early were found out and rejected. The information that family members, especially Hans von Dohnanyi and Rüdiger Schleicher, brought with them from their spheres of professional activity made quite plain the baseness of the system and the danger bound up with it.

The tasks the individual members of the family assumed in the struggle against the system were for each different, according to the profession and personality involved; all were in danger.

Rüdiger Schleicher did not take an active part in plans for the direct execution of the overthrow. But he knew of such plans, approved them fully, and directly helped those involved with his advice. He let himself be included in the preparations for the administration to be set up after a successful overthrow. A more intimate exchange of ideas, concerning questions of the future organization in the sphere of aviation, existed with his brother-in-law Klaus Bonhoeffer. To his assistant in the Institute for the Law of the Air, Dr. Hans John, who later was condemned and died together with him, he gave opportunities for conspiratorial journeys and in addition made available his rooms at the Institute and his house for the appropriate conferences.

In October 1944, Rüdiger Schleicher was arrested and handcuffed and interrogated for weeks at a time. The constant threats of reprisal against his wife and children and the idea that their fate depended on his statements burdened him more than did his own situation. In the interrogations, he named the deprivation of rights, the persecution of the Jews, the action against the church and "enemies of the state," and the construction of the concentration camps as decisive motives for his resistance activities. His direct participation in the proceedings of 20 July 1944 could not be proved. His knowledge of the existence of plans for a *Putsch* and his rejection of the regime, which, as he declared, had to be brought down in the interest of the Reich—if necessary through the removal of Hitler—as well as the fact that he was ready to assume definite responsibilities after the overthrow, were sufficient reasons for the death sentence.

His son-in-law Eberhard Bethge, who was with him in prison and who was the only one of the imprisoned family members who survived, later reported to the family how my father bore his fate. Here are some excerpts from the report from 1945:

"In this hard time, a few of Father's more warm-hearted prison guards had suspected and had discovered what kind of a man they had before them. The circle of those who spent a large part of their watch time in front of cells 269 and 270 [belonging to Klaus Bonhoeffer and Rüdiger Schleicher] grew immediately. . . . Father took an interest in each individual and quickly was fully informed about the origins and interests of the young so-called *volksdeutschen*[3] SS men. With one of them, he studied, guided by maps, all the beautiful places he still wanted to see in peacetime with his conversation partner. He had another tell him with what customs a Swabian wedding

---

3. [This adjective has the meaning of "belonging to the German *Volk*." Yet, here there are considerable difficulties with *Volk*, which carries the meaning of "nation," "people," "folk," "race," and "ethnic group." None of these renderings alone is sufficient but all must be included when attempting to understand the adjective, especially in the National Socialist context.]

was celebrated in Hungary or Siebenbürgen. There were many who spoke in front of me with effusive enthusiasm about number 270, about Father's warm-hearted goodness and interestedness, about the selflessness with which he gave to his fellow prisoners from his packages. In this, above all, it was reported to me, no one in the entire building surpassed him. The young SS men, with all their acquired insensibility and schooling, still had not lost the distinct feeling for the way one could make the best of a bad situation.

"All of this certainly explains why, in December, the violin suddenly resounded through the hall—an event without parallel in Lehrter Street. . . . So the guards each time opened his door, and the gigantic hall carried the sound through our entire B wing. The guards requested *Lieder* and current hit songs; Father played the old folk songs, one after the other. . . . The trio and quartet themes, the sonatas and oratorio melodies that Father had ready in his memory in such abundance seemed to be even more beautiful and fuller than outside. . . .

"Then came the wretched day [of the judgment]. . . . As Father caught sight of me and I felt completely helpless in the face of the event, he winked at me affably and smiled so heartily that I was completely bewildered. . . .

"The general opinion was that no one walked around the prison yard in such an unbroken and upright manner, that no one greeted the others so amiably and with such a warm smile all the time as did Father. . . . He certainly felt himself responsible for the inner and outer bearing of his fellow victims of misfortune and was now . . . the support for many others, free and easy, helpful and consoling."

His death sentence on 2 February 1945 was the last judgment from the notorious president of the People's Tribunal, Roland Freisler; the following day Freisler was killed by a bomb in an air raid. There followed now a struggle to gain time, the desperate attempt to delay until the end of the war the execution of the judgment, not yet signed, by means of a retrial of the case and petitions for mercy. All efforts were to no avail; in the night of 22–23 April, as the Russian army already stood on the outskirts of Berlin and the thunder of the guns could already be heard, Rüdiger Schleicher died near his prison from a shot through the head, together with Klaus Bonhoeffer, Hans John, Friedrich Justus Perels, and others.

Hans-Walter Schleicher

[Approved Letter]

Berlin
[Lehrter Street 3]
29 December 1944

My dearest Ursel,

Many thanks for your dear letter, which has made me very happy. How splendid that you have celebrated so nicely even without me and that little Dietrich let all of you forget your cares somewhat. Also, that the parents were with you and are healthy pleases me very much. To dear Mama an early heartfelt birthday wish: may she and Papa be permitted to experience in good health the return of better times. And now for you, for the new year, everything that could possibly bring inner and outer happiness. Thank you for your tremendous love and care for me; I know and constantly feel how you think about me and worry about me. I never would have thought that I could ever cause you to worry so much; I myself am again and again unhappy about that. Above all, stay healthy and keep your wonderful composure and strength. In addition, you must, above all, nourish yourself well. Please now, really, don't send me so much to eat; as much as I would like to, I can never manage all of it and always have to give away a part of it, which I regret for your sakes.

I have enjoyed enormously your marvelous Christmas things: your vest and shoes; Tine's[4] socks; your and Renate's[5] baked goods; Dodo's[6] tobacco; Hans-Walter's[7] cigars and, above all, his personal greeting; your delightful pictures; the little tree and the azalea; and

---

4. Daughter Christine. [Notes without brackets are by the editors.—TRANS.]
5. Daughter Renate.
6. Daughter Dorothee.
7. Son Hans-Walter, in the *Luftwaffe* at the front.

everything else that came, above all, Klaus's[8] fine calendar. For all of this, I can only thank you and ask you to pass along my thanks. I know what effort went into all of it, especially from you and Tine. . . .

My day begins with calisthenics, then, if possible, working (not purely reading) activity until noon, and in the late afternoon more light reading. I have worked through a book of physics and one on harmony, but I would like more from the more popular physics, mathematics, and astronomy books of Hans-Walter's.

Other book requests: Delbrück's *Weltgeschichte* (gradually), also more from Ranke; further, my *Sachsenspiegel* (Reclam booklet) and the small German legal history (two small Göschen volumes), perhaps a larger work on the subject from the Institute.[9]

And now I think lovingly of each one of you—of Hans-Walter, that he may return to us in good health; of Renate, that her cares about her own dear husband may be dispelled quickly and happily (in the yard during exercise period, I rejoice again and again over his vigor); of Dodo and Tine and their vocational and school cares; of your brothers and sisters and my brother, that everything may go well, as well as for our entire German *Volk*.

In love and thankfulness, I embrace you, treasure of my heart.

Your Rüdiger

[Approved Letter]

Berlin
[Lehrter Street 3]
30 January 1945

My dear Ursel,
So this is now my letter for the anniversary of our engagement on

---

8. The godson, Klaus von Dohnanyi.
9. [Rüdiger Schleicher refers here to the five-volume *World History* of Hans Delbrück (1848–1929). He also requested his copy of the oldest, most influential book of German law from the Middle Ages, the *Sachsenspiegel*, which he possessed in the inexpensive edition from the publishing house Reclam. His volumes of legal history were published by Göschen.]

February 5; I hope it arrives in time and finds you at ease about our future—or at ease at least to some degree. The fate of all German people today is indeed uncertain in view of the events of the war; we indeed do not stand here alone. I myself am reassured by the fact that I know you are in good health and, above all, are secure with your parents, that you can have the girls with you, and that our little grandson, whose first birthday now, of course, is also just around the corner, is like a little good-luck charm for you in the house. That is really the main thing in all this distress. Just take care that the parents keep you going; that they are properly fed and have the necessary rest. They are now truly indeed your rod and staff—as they indeed have at other times been for us in our twenty-two years together.

Beginning with our engagement and the first days of our marriage, up to the present day! Yes, there I am in the midst of all the beauty you have created and given to me: in our wonderful home with its cozy dining room, where we all were together at mealtimes around our constantly growing round table; or in our sun-filled living room with its delightful furniture and pleasing pictures, where we sang and made music together on Sunday; or at our wonderful birthday, or family, celebrations; or in the comfortable little Friedrichsbrunn house, where we first began our married life and where you cooked for me the first time, where Hans-Walter spoke his first words and learned to walk, and where everything is full of pleasant memories; or at some other holiday resort, in Tempelburg or Eisenbach, on Kniebis, in Deep, or Langeoog, or even that time in Lugano; or even in Tübingen or Stuttgart or wherever we have spent wonderful, happy hours together, with or without the children. . . . Everywhere and again and again, you have made it wonderful for me. Thank you for everything, and don't lose hope that the sunshine will come again after the rain that has broken out over us. We think with great confidence of our Hans-Walter too, who really has a heavy responsibility out there; and our daughters should remain courageous, keep their cheerfulness, and Eberhard, too, should be permitted to return again soon to Renate.

So now, I myself have got a feeling of happiness again because of this letter; that does me a lot of good, although otherwise I am calm and suffer no privation of any kind in my cell. Farewell, my dearest. I

kiss you, and greet you and the children and parents from the bottom
of my heart.

Your Rüdiger

31 January, morning. All my love, my dear; accept this greeting of
good morning, too!

[Ursula Schleicher to her son Hans-Walter, after the death sentence
pronounced against his father]

[Marienburger Allee 42]
9 February 1945

My dear good boy,
    You'll be surprised that I have not written you since Thursday. I have
written two letters, but it broke my heart to send them. But, after all,
you are now indeed a man and are able to find comfort and strength in
the faith given to us. On 2 February Freisler condemned Father, Uncle
Klaus, John, and Perels to death, and Harnack a day before. Even the
court-appointed attorneys with Father are baffled; Weimann as well as
Neubert can't comprehend it. But the judgment cannot be reversed. I
was at the People's Tribunal on the third, early in the morning, and I
said to the Reich solicitor-general that they would spill innocent blood
if that judgment was carried out and that that would be avenged. He
said, "Madam, I understand your agitation, but I don't want to hear
such talk here." I said, "I suppose so, but that's the way it is!" There-
upon there was a full alarm. I went to the cellar in Father's Institute.
Then came this terrible attack. Although where we were the back of
the house was torn away and bomb after bomb fell—everything
shook, the stucco fell off, water came into the neighboring cellar—an
attack has never left me so cold; I only thought, If it would only hit the
right ones! At the time of the attack, Uncle Rolf,[10] who by chance had
come on the second and wanted to help, was below in the subway at
Potsdamer Platz. He saw then, as we did too when we came out, that

10. The Stuttgart brother, Dr. Rolf Schleicher, who was at that time staff surgeon.

the People's Tribunal building was burning, and he rushed over to it. He was called, as the first doctor, to the dying Freisler. When he was asked about his personal data, he said, "I am the brother of the one who was innocently condemned to death yesterday by this man." Whereupon, a clear and, according to some, an articulated horror seized those who were standing around. The judgment, as things now stand, has not yet been signed by Freisler, since the hearing ended only at seven o'clock on the second. That delays the case, especially since the files perhaps were burned up too. Usually they go to the Justice Ministry the day after, and yesterday they were not yet there. The only thing that can help is to gain time. That Germany should yet be robbed by violence of such men as Father was, is unbelievable and a disgrace for the leading men. Father is charged with not making a denunciation. If what Uncle Klaus is charged with is true, should he have denounced him? No, better dead!

I was able to speak with Father on the twenty-second anniversary of our engagement day (5 February); Dorothee was there, too. He was calm, composed, and said that it is an egoism to leave this present world, and that the only thing hard for him would be to leave us behind. He has, however, also filed a petition for mercy because of us. Whether justly or unjustly condemned, he said, does not matter; they suffer a common fate. He asked for art books, a piano score of the Saint Matthew Passion and the B-minor Mass. He wants to occupy himself only with art and religious things. Harnack, who sits next to him, yesterday told his wife that it had given him such strength the day before to have heard the Saint Matthew Passion played the whole day.[11] How thankful we must be that he has that. Father wrote yesterday, "I am doing well; if only I could know the same about you too." As we took leave of each other on 5 February, Father said too, "Perhaps, after all, twenty-two more years will be granted to us." We, too, must not lose our courage. Time flies, and perhaps someone still will see once again that these men are not criminals deserving death. It rests in God's hand. If it is intended for them, then God will preserve

11. Through the help of one of the two commandants, it was possible to bring Rüdiger Schleicher's violin to him in his cell.

them from something worse. I was quite calm when I had seen Father; now, they say, one is supposed to get permission to visit every eight days. Who knows when you will receive this letter? You've got it the hardest because you must deal with this sorrow alone. But you can be proud of your father, and this consciousness strengthens us, for, of the court that condemned Father, none are worthy of loosening his shoe-laces, but they are blinded and can't do anything about it; they don't know what human greatness is. The court trying Father, to the very last one of them, behaves in a cowardly way. I'd like to make them too realize their miserable pettiness one day. Germany's men fall at the front or are whisked off violently to death: what is left?

Now, my good boy, keep your faith in spite of everything. It gives us strength and confidence and binds us together, even when we are separated. How long the letters take I don't know, since we don't as yet have an acknowledgment from you of our letters.

Father sends you his very best greetings; you should stay of good cheer, as he does too.

Farewell, my darling; keep your chin up!

Love, your mother

Early on the second, I brought Father a breakfast in prison. We waited until they were led out. All handcuffed. Father came up to me, gave me a kiss, and said, "Be of good cheer!" They yelled at him, but it was too late. Then, from out of the horrible Black Maria [prisoners' auto] resounded his Hedgehog whistle. That was how confident he was.

[Approved Letter to the Field]

Berlin
[Lehrter Street 3]
14 February 1945

My dear Hans-Walter,

In a week's time, you'll have your twenty-first birthday. You cele-brate it in a difficult time, in the midst of a responsible mission and burdened with concern for my fate and for that of Mother and your sisters. Perhaps it will seem too hard for you. Here, I'd like to wish you today all the more happiness, and to say to you first of all: Stay of good cheer; don't let yourself be influenced in your service, nor in your behavior toward other people, but rather, stay the way you were in the past: honorable, kind-hearted, and ready to do any task for which you're needed. That is now the main thing.

Don't be worried about me. The petition for mercy is still being considered, but even apart from that, I have had a tremendously beautiful and happy life. It was best at home, thanks to Mother's love, but also thanks to you children who gave me only gladness. Therefore, I can also only say to you generally, Continue to go your own way just as you have begun it; remain true to yourself; then nothing can go wrong, not even in your service and in your wonderful profession, into the fundamentals of which I have, you know, gone somewhat here (I have also read two chemical books here). That you must hold fast to music is something that I don't especially need to tell you; here, too, I have felt again and again what it means to me as I "read through" the piano score of the Saint Matthew Passion and the B-minor Mass. That goes quite well with the memories, too.

In front of me stands your nice picture next to that of your sisters, while that of your mother hangs above them. So I have all of you in front of me. From the bottom of my heart, I wish for you that you withstand every hazard in good health and can be a strong support for Mother and your sisters if I should no longer be.

Personally, I am doing well; I am calm and am reading as in the past. Yesterday, I had permission to speak with Mother and Christine; that was a great pleasure for me. Mother told me too about your recent difficult flight.[12] Today, by the way, is my mother's seventy-second birthday; this makes me too think back with thankfulness to my own parents' house in dear old Stuttgart. You too keep your love for Swabia!

And now I shake your hand, and greet you, in love.

Your father

12. Crash during combat duty.

[Evidently a Secret Message]

Berlin
[Lehrter Street 3]
18 March 1945

My dearest darling,

It is Sunday morning and it may be about eleven o'clock, and you should get a greeting from me just so you know how I am doing and are not unhappy because of me, perhaps thinking that I am in a bad way or that I am sitting in my cell freezing and depressed. There's nothing of all that!

I've made for myself a wonderful worship service—or more correctly, not *I* for myself, but rather, if I may say so, God himself makes something like that, so that one really becomes perfectly calm and elevated beyond all things. I have read, first of all, the Bible passages for this Sunday that are in the hymnal, and in the devotional watchwords—especially Psalms 42 and 43, but then also a few others. In the process, I have also come across the last—twenty-ninth—chapter of 1 Chronicles and the beginning chapters of 2 Chronicles, nothing but astonishingly beautiful and powerful things, or at least astonishing things. Then I have read the marvelous hymns 219 ("Gib dich zufrieden") and 209—are not verses 9 and 10 of 219 beautiful beyond all measure? And then I have played these and other hymns on the violin—also, of course, "Was mein Gott will" and "Wenn wir in höchsten Nöten sein" (210 and 211)—and that has led me again right into the midst of the Saint Matthew Passion, from which I can play on the violin not merely my favorite aria "Erbarme Dich" (p. 92) but also "Er hat uns allen wohlgetan" and "Aus Liebe will mein Heiland sterben" (p. 109), some chorales, and the unbelievable concluding chorus "Wie setzen uns mit Tränen nieder," so that I have the greatest pleasure from it. You see, I lack nothing. And you can be sure that, in the process, I not only begin to feel spiritually well but I also become physically warm. From my table and the wall, your dear pictures look at me, and in addition, the Collegiate Church in Stuttgart and the Hölderlin Tower in Tübingen in Schäfer's pretty watercolor, and your yellow narcissus—they are still blooming, too—and everything is right and good and, what is more, no one can take these things away from me; neither can anyone take all of you away from me. So, my darling, don't let all of your hearts become burdened on account of all the misfortune and misery, but rather stay strong and confident. I hope you hear from Hans-Walter again soon; he really still can't be at his original place but certainly has been led back farther. Because of that, no one will have heard anything from him for so long a time.

And what else? In the last week I have read all the letters—epistles—of the New Testament, part of them in comparison with the Greek text, and on the whole, I was not very satisfied by it. The translation there is not satisfying, but the content, too, really doesn't touch one deeply. The Psalms, Proverbs, Ecclesiastes, Isaiah 40 and following are, on the other hand, something completely different; the "exclusively essential" in religion is still the "relationship to God," if you will: prayer and the attitude that grows out of it. All the often-convoluted explanations, evidence of Jesus' significance, his sacrificial death, his office as high priest, etc., in the epistles really become very unimportant here. Even a book like Seneca's marvelous aphorisms, which show a very high ethical and religious attitude, in my opinion stands above most of these epistles, which really are somewhat fanatical, in part, and partly primitive—disregarding the strongly mystical translation which always speaks about prophets, saints, etc., where one certainly must put more simply a preacher, a believer, etc.

In the meantime, the big attack took place, which could be endured in our cellar with a feeling of complete security. I hope it turned out as well for all of you, too!

Otherwise, I am still working on Delbrück's *Weltgeschichte*, which I am reading together with Mommsen's *Römischer Geschichte*—that too is marvelously colorful and delightful. Then, after that, comes Stifter's *Nachsommer*, which attracts me again and again, and Reuter's *Festungstid*,[13] in a way my lightest reading, which I read with complete pleasure while comparing it with my own present situation: R. too was once condemned to death! So you see me busy the whole day; and in between, a good meal and an ample sleep, which are followed by a

---

13. [The works mentioned here by Rüdiger Schleicher are the *History of Rome*, by Theodor Mommsen (1817–1903), the three-volume novel *Nachsommer* (Indian summer), by Adalbert Stifter (1805–68), and the volume of reminiscences *Ut mine Festungstid* (From my time of imprisonment), by Fritz Reuter (1810–74).]

daily cold washing and gymnastic exercises, complete for you my existence, which, apart from the fact of my imprisonment, has nothing
oppressive about it. Therefore, don't all of you be worried about me,
but think more about yourselves, about whom I alone ought to worry—
but to worry without being able to act is a very dumb thing.

If you could leave, you should not be held here out of consideration
of me. Who knows whether we too still will not be taken away. I
assume, then, that you will go to Rolf at Niedernau, or perhaps to
Friedrichsbrunn?

Lovingly I think of you all, especially of you, my darling! What heavy
cares you have to bear now; only take care of yourself, too, and eat
enough. Yesterday, you were very thin and small. And now I clasp you
to my heart in tender love; thank you for everything; greet the children, the parents, brothers, siblings, and friends.

Your Rüdiger

March 20. Be sure not to send this letter to Hans-Walter with the post.
Also yesterday and today I have been well. I have read *Nachsommer* to
the end; the last chapter is simply wonderful. The snowdrops are delightful. By the way, your place in heaven is certainly better than mine;
really, absolutely no one can be kinder and better and more consider-
ate and truer than you, my darling.

[Approved Letter?]
[To Professor Karl Bonhoeffer]

Lehrter Street Prison
30 March 1945

Dear Papa,

This time you are celebrating your birthday at a point in time when
we believe that the distress of the German *Volk* could hardly become
greater and that the crisis is moving toward its decisive moment. At the
same time, you see almost all the men of your family in danger and all
other members in severe anguish and concern about them. That is for
you and Mama a burden that certainly surpasses everything you have
ever before experienced. But, at the same time, it is the concern that

maintains you both and gives you your strength. And it is our greatest wish that this strength may be preserved for you both as long as it is at all possible and conceivable. Your infinite goodness and calm—and if it is permitted for me to say it—your wisdom, combined with the untiring care and all-considering energy of Mama, is, after all, that which today visibly and invisibly sustains, guides, or at least, accompanies all of us, your children, your sons- and daughters-in-law, and your grandchildren. If today, in spite of everything I have experienced, I sit in my cell with a calm heart and know that Ursel and the children are secure in spite of everything, then it is so because both of you stand in the background with all your love, and I can only thank both of you from the bottom of my heart for that. I am very sorry, and at the beginning I suffered a great deal because of it, that I became a cause for worry for you as well. And I know how Ursel is weighed down by this fate. But I believe from the very bottom of my heart that it still will have a favorable end, not for me alone, but for Klaus and the others concerned as well, even Dietrich and Hans. Lovingly, I think too of Hans-Walter, who like little Klaus now is in the midst of a difficult mission. I hope you will hear good things from them for your birthday and that all will continue to remain good.

That Eberhard, who looks after me every day with his delightfully happy disposition, will return home to you happy and again in good health, is something I really cannot doubt at all. And may all the others who belong to the family also remain well and survive in complete good health everything still to come. I myself have you and Mama, too, to thank besides for much love and care and also patience. Please accept this written thanks today in the hope that I will be able to do it orally, too. Among the joys for which I have you to thank here belongs the constantly astonishing splendid provision of tobacco. I hope it doesn't impose too great a sacrifice on you. But I can see, not only from the containers, that many a delicious dish that Ursel brings comes from your kitchen. And for this too, I thank you both. But stop now, especially Ursel too—don't send me so much. Ursel is sick now and needs it herself more than I, who, after all, hardly move and really only read, even if not just entertainment books, still only what the heart desires and therefore what is always filled with excitement and satisfaction. At the present time, Delbrück's really beautiful *Weltgeschichte* is in the foreground, and I've got as far as the Ottomans. "Reckless-ness" (thoughtlessness, guilt) as a legal problem—and its reverse (re-pentance, conscience, punishment)—should soon occupy me again. And also other things in consideration of today's technical occupations, for example, that of the airplane pilot, where the smallest failure can lead to the most grievous consequences and where the necessity of complete exemption from sweeping liability for guilt in cases of only *slight* recklessness is always in my mind, because this simply will not be separable from excusable failure. Can I someday read something psy-chological about this from your books? Ursel already told me that you thought you didn't have anything about this, but I couldn't, after all, explain the problem to her so quickly.

Now, from the bottom of my heart, I wish you and Mama and everyone a splendid birthday and a calm Easter season full of joyful memories of earlier wonderful family celebrations, especially of your seventy-fifth birthday. And now I greet you in grateful love as

Your faithful Rüdiger

[Approved Letter]

Berlin
[Lehrter Street 3]
1 April 1945

Dearest Darling, dear Children,

Today you should receive still another special Easter letter, after I could not, as you know, see you yesterday (a few days more will pass before that will be possible). From the bottom of my heart, I wish all of you a wonderful day. I know that you are celebrating in the air raid cellar and it is even more like war than usual; you are nevertheless spiritually happy, and that is the most important thing. Or, is it not so? . . . You know, surely, that I am doing well; I have your two marvelous bouquets standing in front of me on the two little tables, above them lies the nest with the Easter eggs, and on the wall behind your pictures is Klaus's saying "Christ is risen from all his agony!" At the same time, I think about the four-voice choral singing we used to enjoy, and I am indeed glad when I can play it on the violin afterwards. But I think too about the unbelievably beautiful passages in the Missa and the B-minor Mass "Et resurrexit," and about the jubilation with which the chorus sings that. And at the same time I think—is it presumptuous?—a little bit about us here and about the belief that we too are permitted to rise again when the time for it has come.

Dear Ursel, stay confident yourself and of good cheer. You don't know how much peace your remark "We are, too" brings me every time; if I know that you are calm, then I am satisfied. But take care of yourself as well as you can; under no circumstances send me too many good things. You have spoiled me beyond all measure recently, you know, and that makes me really unhappy, because I know that you have less.

And now, a kiss to each of you, and to you, my darling, a special one.

All my love,

Father

[Approved Letter]

[Lehrter Street 3]
13 April 1945

Dearest Ursel,

First of all, thank you for your love, which surrounds me at every turn and also strengthens me internally in my existence, The consciousness that you are here and that you help me gives me the greatest strength. I hope everything isn't beyond your strength—Tine[14]and I and Hans-Walter and the constant airplane attacks. What you have to bear is really tremendous. And yet we must be happy and thankful that everything up to now has occurred the way it has, and, with you, I am of the firm belief that everything will still be well and that the present time has been of use for me. I have got away from my restless haste and activity, and again got used to calm and concentration; how really pleasant it is to be able to read a work like Delbrück through very thoroughly and systematically. Of course, most of the time I finish no

14. Christine had had an accident.

more than eighty pages a day, often only fifty or sixty, but that's good enough. In addition, there are the daily walks, once or twice and as long as an hour; a little bit of violin; reading in the Old Testament—at the present time the Psalms one after the other—or in Marcus Aurelius's very beautiful meditations, occasionally Gottfried Keller, too, and regularly the newspaper. So the day passes quite well and quickly. I am in bed most nights at eight o'clock (or even earlier) until six-thirty, thus enough time and rest in spite of the disturbing alarms. The food here has fallen into short supply, and those who are dependent on only what there is here can be sorry. Thank you for your very wonderful food, which couldn't be better and more abundant; only, be careful that all of you keep enough. Hans-Walter's letter, by the way, is very delightful and shows a great maturity; greet him ever so heartily for me. . . . I hope that Dorothee need not report for duty; I assume, though, that so many workers elsewhere have been released that they will not have recourse to a sixteen-year-old.

I embrace you tenderly; greet Tine especially too.

Your husband

KLAUS
BONHOEFFER

Born 5 January 1901 in Breslau—1918, at the Western Front as a seventeen-year-old—after legal studies in Tübingen and Heidelberg, doctorate in Berlin—resided in Geneva, Amsterdam, and England for the study of international law—1930, marriage to Emmi Delbrück; at the same time, settlement in Berlin as a lawyer—corporation counsel, finally chief corporation counsel, for German Lufthansa—early contacts in the political resistance—arrested 1 October 1944—condemned to death 2 February 1945—shot 23 April 1945.

Reminiscence

Klaus Bonhoeffer, born 5 January 1901 in Breslau, was the third of eight children. His father, the psychiatrist Karl Bonhoeffer, at that time supervised the observation ward for mentally ill prisoners at the penitentiary there. His mother was a daughter of the Potsdam court chaplain and later Breslau theology professor Karl Alfred von Hase. She had passed her teacher's examination (that was considered emancipated at that time) and spared all eight children their first three school years since she instructed them all herself—in each case along with several neighbor children.

His oldest brother, Karl-Friedrich, the physical chemist, wrote down the following about Klaus in 1953:

"When my brother Klaus was three years old, our father wrote in his yearbook, 'Klaus is a careful, quiet, realistic observer . . . a droll, fat little rascal,' and later, 'Klaus thinks his own thoughts,' and after a few more years, 'He is still the philosopher and thinks over the problems of life.' In the crush of two older and five younger siblings with whom he grew up, he quite early created a world for himself: he learned to knit, was quite skilled at handicrafts, had a lot of fun with the microscope, and enthusiastically took photographs for a time. He was considered the most musical among us children, played cello well for a boy of his age, and still later, as a mature man, loved to make music in his family with his children. Full of good humor and original practical jokes, he nevertheless really did not have an easygoing temperament. The love of our mother, therefore, went out to him in a special way, and he was just as devoted to her. As goodhearted as he was, he could be equally recalcitrant when treated wrongly. His teachers and superiors had a hard time with him. It was impossible for him to submit to the will of a subordinate spirit. As a school boy and later in life up to the end, he was not afraid of the battle that thus resulted for him again and again. I have known no person who let his eye for human quality be clouded so little by age or rank as he did. It was therefore natural that he saw through the low standards of rising National Socialism and when it had gained power was not intimidated or bewildered by it.

"When he was sixteen or seventeen, those interests began to grasp my brother which gave content to his later life—the problems of living together in human society. As a schoolboy still, he got himself Marx's *Kapital* and devoted much time and effort to its study. Later, it was Max Weber's *Religionssoziologie*, Tönnies's *Gemeinschaft und Gesellschaft*, and Kropotkin's *Gegenseitige Hilfe in der Entwicklung*,[1] for example, that occupied him and that I as an older brother got to know through him. In his sociological interests, there also emerged points

1. [Klaus Bonhoeffer's youthful reading encompassed not only Karl Marx's well-known *Capital* but also Max Weber's *Sociology of Religion*, Ferdinand Tönnies's *Community and Society*, and Peter Kropotkin's *Mutual Aid: A Factor of Evolution*.]

of contact with his theology-studying younger brother Dietrich, who at that time was working on his *Communio Sanctorum* (1927). In his legal studies, it was not the formal and abstract constructions that captivated my brother Klaus but rather the human and social functions of the law. How much this is expressed in his writings about the factory-councils law and the 'Meistbegünstigung im modernen Völkerrecht' (1930) I do not know. But it certainly is expressed in the essay on the 'Grundformen des Rechts' in the *Weissen Blätter* (1942),[2] in spite of the camouflage necessary at that time. He was a man with a passionate sense of justice. That drove him into conflict.

"The older he became the more his interests broadened. He used every opportunity that presented itself to become acquainted with foreign lands, and he was able to tell in an uncommonly lively manner about his travel experiences and about the life style of foreign peoples. His study trips and professional travels led him from Finland to North Africa, from England to Greece and Turkey, often under the most primitive conditions. But his love was reserved for the countries with a Latin culture, France, Italy, and Spain, and for the French language. He had an unusual joy in discovering and collecting beautiful and characteristic pieces of art and history. While it was primarily human and cultural things that interested him on his journeys, he also, in the process, developed an eye for Germany's foreign political possibilities, and he perceived the blindness of the National Socialist movement as it headed toward power.

"His lifelong friend was Justus Delbrück, whose younger sister Emmi, the love of his youth, he married. He was a very kind father to his children and paid intense attention to their education. In tranquil times, he never would have gone into politics. During his life, he remained too much the philosopher to be bothered with outward ambition. Also, he did not have an easy command of extemporaneous speech. But he could not sit idly by and see how everything that made life worth living for him—law, culture, and the honor of his *Volk*—was disgraced by an inferior class of upstarts, and so he partici-

2. [Klaus Bonhoeffer's treatise in 1930 dealt with "Most-Favored Nation Status in Modern International Law." His essay on "Basic Forms of the Law" appeared in 1942 in the journal *White Pages*.]

pated in the preparations for the overthrow of Hitler. By means of connections that he had through his brother-in-law Hans von Doh-nanyi to Beck and Goerdeler, through his wife's cousin Ernst von Harnack to men in the Social Democratic Party and the old unions, through our brother Dietrich to the Confessing Church and the ecumenical movement, through Otto John to Prince Louis Ferdinand, he systematically created important lateral connections between the various resistance groups.

"When he saw that his arrest was imminent, he did not flee, because he did not want to burden his relatives and friends. He bore the tortures of the Gestapo in the consciousness that he was fighting the good fight. Condemned to death, he said to me during a visit in the prison that he needed nothing more there, that he had, after all, the Saint Matthew Passion with him. And as I replied that it was really wonderful that he could hear the music while reading through it, he said, 'Yes, but the text, too! The text!'

"On his grave in the Dorotheenstadt Cemetery in Berlin, where he rests with a number of fellow prisoners and many victims of the last days of the war, lies a stone with the words 'Blessed are they who are persecuted for righteousness' sake, for theirs is the kingdom of heaven.' "

To this picture from the pen of the older brother, which in its warmth and concurrent soberness is characteristic of the writer of it as well as of the one written about, I would like to add only a few words.

After his father in 1912 followed a call to the Charité in Berlin, and after the family in 1918 had moved out of the city to Wangenheim Street in Grunewald, we became neighbors. There were seven of us Delbrück brothers and sisters, and immediately there emerged friendships during hiking and ice skating and while playing music together. Klaus with his cello, his five-years-younger brother Dietrich on the piano, and I with the violin—we captured for ourselves the paths into classical chamber music. The circle immediately widened with the addition of the new brother-in-law Rüdiger Schleicher as violinist, and my cousin Ernst von Harnack as flutist. I mention this because later these musical evenings became the camouflage for many conspiratorial meetings.

In 1920–21, Klaus studied law together with my brother Justus in Tübingen and Heidelberg. They hiked a great deal. Klaus said at that time in reference to Justus, "Understanding and character grow so seldom on the same branch." A passionate and a contemplative temperament had found one another.

Both in these years observed with dismay the undiminished reactionary tendencies among students and among professors, and above all the behavior of students when an instructor dared for once to say something positive about the young republic. A member of the "Schwaben" students' corps was forbidden to greet his young Jewish friends (Heidelberg, 1921). Klaus's letters home and to his future brother-in-law Hans von Dohnanyi contain gloomy forecasts for Germany's political future, and already the presentiment that people might have to act together against it.

These letters, though, also mirror the abundance of that which he absorbed on his way and the adventures that happened to him. Starting from Geneva, where he made inquiries at the League of Nations, he visited his brother Dietrich in Spain. At the flea market in Madrid, he found a signed Picasso for a few pesetas. The authenticity of the picture was then actually confirmed by experts. Later, he once threatened Dietrich that he wouldn't get any more mail from him if he continued to run down bullfighting.

At the time of our marriage in 1930, Klaus became a lawyer in Berlin, later corporation counsel, and finally chief corporation counsel, for German Lufthansa AG. His indispensable assistant, especially in the political activities that began immediately, in the finding and bringing together of like-minded individuals, and in planning and pressing forward with those plans, was at that time Dr. Otto John. This man's brother Hans John was later an assistant to Rüdiger Schleicher in the Institute for the Law of the Air at the university.

In the meantime, the net around the citizen was spun ever more tightly through the extended activities of the Secret State Police[3] in the inspection of letters and the surveillance of telephone conversations, visits from block wardens, etc., so that all the work could take place only at night and under concealment. (I remember that we

3. [The Secret State Police were the **Ge**heime **Sta**atspo**l**izei, or Gestapo.]

once spent half a month's salary for a pound of coffee.) For this reason, the words "resistance movement" common today are misleading. A movement with demonstrations, enlightening articles, proclamations, information, etc., was really out of the question.

We knew more about breaches of the law and atrocities by the National Socialists than did others, through Hans von Dohnanyi's position with the justice minister. But Klaus energetically forbade me to spread this knowledge about, because that would only provoke our arrest: "Please understand, a dictatorship is a snake. When you step on its tail, it bites you. You have to strike the head, and only the military can do that, for it has the access to Hitler and the weapons. The only thing that makes sense to do is to convince the military that they must act." His entire work, as his brother Karl-Friedrich has described it, was dedicated to this goal. But it was important at the same time to prepare for "afterwards." The different social groups at the given moment, that is, after a successful assassination attempt upon Hitler, had to be able to act in coordination. It was a matter of attempting to make military action politically possible for the hesitating generals. But the hopes proved deceptive again and again.

In that November night in 1938 as the synagogues burned,[4] he saw a general with broad red stripes down his pants who looked away and walked by. Before he told me this, he asked me in a tone of despairing bitterness, "What is this: little head, big beak, long red legs, stands with his feet in the mire? A stork? A German general!"

Under the impress of Hitler's breaches of the law, which simply were accepted by the citizens, he outlined a textbook about fundamental concepts of the law. The manuscript was destroyed by fire in a night bomb attack along with everything else.

On 6 April 1943, Hans von Dohnanyi, his wife Christine (Klaus's sister), and Dietrich, the younger brother, were arrested and could no longer share in the work. Thus Klaus's agitation and activities increased to the utmost. The hope for a final act by the generals was his very life breath. On 20 July 1944, Stauffenberg finally attempted it— and failed.

---

4. [Meant here is the night of 9–10 November 1938, the *Kristallnacht,* in which the National Socialists organized a pogrom against synagogues and Jewish businesses throughout Germany.]

On 1 October 1944, Klaus was arrested in the house of his sister Ursula Schleicher, while I, with the children, was staying with relatives in Holstein because of the bombs. We could have hidden him there with a fisherman. He didn't want that, because he feared that then his parents or the children and I would be taken as hostages.

On 2 February 1945, he was condemned to death along with his brother-in-law Schleicher and Hans John. On the evening of the same day, Justus, who had his cell on the third floor, saw him as the prisoners stepped forward in the opened doors of their individual cells to receive their food. With a look and that attitude which says more than words can do, he sent his greetings up to him.

On 23 April, they murdered him together with Rüdiger Schleicher, Hans John, Justus Perels, and others. Justus Delbrück saw freedom again—for three weeks. Then the Russians took him to a detention camp at Lieberose, in the Lausitz. He died there half a year later from diphtheria.

Emmi Bonhoeffer

[Berlin, Alte Allee 11]
Monday, 19 July 1944

Dear Walter,[5]

I thank you very much for your letter which you have dictated to Mama. It is certainly very nice where you are, and I already am very happy to be able to visit you. Where would you rather be, in the forest or at the sea? Have you already put your feet in the water? Have you ever watched the fishermen when they bring in the fish? Do the fish really freeze in the water when there is no heat in the winter? Are they really in the water because they are so thirsty? You must look in the hedges for the birds. I have seen a lot of butcher birds there. When they kill more bugs than they can eat, they impale them on the thorns. Then they have their own pantry; I've already seen that many times. Here in the garden it's very nice now. There are really a lot of strawber-

---

5. Son Walter.

ries and cherries. Unfortunately, the thrushes eat so many cherries. But, they sing so beautifully in the mornings and evenings, perhaps a song about the cherry tree. That's why I don't want to do anything to them. Are you singing nice new songs too? Do you all sing every evening? I almost believe that all of you will be here again for Christmas. But before that, you will have a birthday. One now cannot yet know whether the war will be over by then. Now, greet Mama, Aunt Lotta,[6] Thomas, and Cornelie,[7] and also your friend and his mother. Write me again soon.

Affectionately,
Your Papa

[Translated from the French:]

[Alte Allee 11]
Wednesday, 21 July 1944

My dear Thomas,

Thank you so much for your letter in French, which I enjoyed very much. I am enclosing a letter from Margot that you ought to answer. Unfortunately, I detect Germanisms that you should not imitate. It appears that your school is quite enjoyable. Anyway, the teacher doesn't fall asleep giving lessons to several classes at once. If you are up to all that is demanded of you, that's to your advantage. I well remember my studies; I could have wished for a teacher who was less pressing, but as I've said, that depends. Mama has written me of your duel with a comrade. I certainly hope that you gave him a good thrashing. One can't always be the strongest—that would even be tiresome. But at the right moment, energy and moral power often produce miracles. I'm sending you a set of airmail stamps. Perhaps you know of someone who would enjoy having them. Personally, I find stamp collecting a bore, but to each his own foolishness.

6. Lotta Carriere.
7. Son and daughter.

I very much hope to come see you soon for a few days.
Then we will play music.
Maybe for a little while we can foget the misery of our days here in
Berlin.
Best wishes,

Papa

3:00 Thursday morning. We've just gone through another alert. All is
well.

[Berlin, Alte Allee 11
undated, 21 or 22 August 1944]

Dearest Emmi, the days with you and the children were like a beautiful dream that will brighten up yet many an hour when I think back to
them. The many good friends you have there are a great comfort to
me. The journey passed bearably. Now I am breathing the aromatic
Berlin air again. I went straight to Ursel, to whom the beans were very
welcome. Rüdiger had just taken up his post again—after his sick
leave. He is now without an assistant in the Institute, since the poor
devil had to be taken away to the sanitarium.[8] Butze's father, too,
now.[9] Poor Agnes[10] has lost her husband. He suffered a stroke. Since
he was bombed out he had not felt well. I have not yet seen my
parents. Papa had an attack of fever. Tomorrow they will come back
from Sackrow.[11] Their condition worries me somewhat. We must continue to believe that all things are to the benefit of those who love
God. So be and stay cheerful, just as your brother does now. Perhaps
music has been given to you just for that purpose. Sing and be thankful
that all of you correctly understand destiny. It is not out of the question
that I will take the rest of my vacation after completion of the meetings
and come once again. I can't as yet be sure about all my plans.

8. Arrest of Hans John.
9. Arrest of Justus Delbrück on 20 August 1944.
10. Agnes von Zahn-Harnack.
11. The von Dohnanyis.

Farewell, all of you! Kiss the children! Thank Lotta for her friendship.
I embrace you.

Your Klaus

Be especially careful with the children. Frau T. is going on vacation for a bit. I will then perhaps, for the time being, also move. Address the mail to Miss Frank.[12]

[Alte Allee 11]
Friday, 8 September 1944

Dearest Emmi,

Thank you very much for your letter from our anniversary. These fourteen years have surely passed quite differently than we should have wished. Other aspects of life determined our happiness. What responsibilities! What insights into the Essential! Earlier it was thought that we had to be an "example" for the children, a role in which I myself have never really believed, a role, after all, that is played preferably by those who are the least suited for it. Today we can be something to the children—even when unexemplary, tarnished—because we have experienced something and, through it, have reached the bottom.

From here there is nothing new to report. I go to work and, besides that, occasionally for a bit in the forest, where I breathe deeply. In the evenings, I visit my parents, but most of the time only very shortly; both of them are really exhausted. It is hardly possible to get news about Hans, but he is lying in a sickward. Christel of course is very troubled. Susi's breast will be operated on tomorrow. It doesn't seem to be anything malignant. I said "nothing new." The standards, as I said, have changed.

Greet the children. I kiss you.

Your Klaus

12. Professor Curtius.

[Approved Letter]

[Lehrter Street 3]
March 1945

Dear Cornelie,

You have made such a pretty calendar for me. Your bookmark too pleases me very much. Those certainly are your most beautiful fairy-tale pictures you have glued on it. Now whenever I open my book, I always think of what my Cornelie might be doing at the moment. Is she doing her schoolwork, is she helping around the house, or is she playing the violin just now? Then my thoughts are with all of you and do not want to leave, just as one does not tear oneself away from a beautiful dream. That is, then, much better than reading. Such a bookmark you have made for me!

The whole winter, sparrows have visited me at my window. Now already, a thrush sings outside mornings and evenings. On my table are catkins Mama brought me. After the uncomfortable winter, perhaps all of you will be looking forward properly to spring for the first time. Just open your eyes and see how it is beginning to rain inconspicuously everywhere. This is the mysterious time. Then, suddenly, it comes powerfully upon us, too, the new life with joy and new courage. Accept it the way it is, and enjoy it with a cheerful heart. It is a gift from heaven. Remember that there are countries that don't know spring. There the people are different too.

If you like to be with Aunt E.[13] so much, why don't you start to draw, too? When she shows you what you do wrong, it will become better immediately and be a lot of fun. You can surprise Mama with it, you know, for her birthday. The eyes glide so easily over something beautiful. Here I even find pleasure now in the view of the prison wall. The upper bricks glow softly in the morning sun, and in the evenings they are a solemn foreground of a distant world. A star shines above it. Then all the gloomy thoughts disappear like fog, and in this peace I whistle to myself in happy remembrance and longing for the past. If only I could do it from the joy of my heart and from thankfulness, like a

13. Elke Wulk.

nightingale. Yes, dear child, learn well to play the violin! You will be very, very happy when you can express yourself there where words are not sufficient.

Here, Mama visits me once a week now and sends me something to eat everyday in my cell along with a nice greeting. I hope you too someday will be so brave and firm in the faith even in the most difficult times. You have such a beautiful name. Have someone tell you some-day about the noble Roman Cornelia.

Now, farewell, my tender Cornelie. Pray that God will give us strength in this distress. It is wonderful that all of you too are reading in the Psalms. You too will have read the bitter story of the Passion and about Easter Sunday. Greet Aunt E. heartily. I kiss you, Thomas, and Walter.

Your Papa

[Approved Letter]

[Lehrter Street 3]
31 March 1945

Dear Parents,

I am addressing this letter for Papa's birthday to you both. The wishes that were never so burning as in this year are meant for the both of you. They are the wishes of the whole family. I almost dare not express the hope that as though through a miracle, the family will emerge intact out of this great general calamity. For a long time it has passed over the people like a natural catastrophe, and nature is of course prodigal. But I believe that the storm over our house will blow over soon. The persecutions will come to an end, and for the survivors of them it will be the way it is for those who dream. My wish and my request are that this peace will do you good for a long time after all this distress, and that you really and truly will enjoy it.

The certainty that a new life will begin again for all of you is so wonderful. My fate too certainly can still turn about suddenly. I am, however, prepared that my life should end soon. These two possibili-ties seem to lie so far apart intellectually that as a human being of flesh and blood, I stagger through hours of weakness despite all the changes in my attitude again and again under the impress of these first days of spring. But I want, after all, not only to live but also just once to make myself felt. Since this surely should occur now through my death, I have also made friends with it. On this ride between death and the devil, death is really a noble companion. The devil conforms himself to the times and certainly has also carried the sword of the cavalier. Thus did the Enlightenment idealize him. The Middle Ages, which also told about his stench, knew him better.

It is in any case a much, much clearer task to die than to live in confused times, for which reason the ones for whom death was determined as a task were always counted fortunate. When I stood at Walter's[14] grave, he always appeared to me to be a fortunate man with the clear line of his life and his early end. Should I still be saved, then I will confront life as a freer human being. Whatever now may come to pass, I am spared a common fate. Emmi understands this, and it certainly will mark the children's path too. For them I wish that they someday can look back upon a wonderful and rich life as thankfully as I do now. It is the life, for which I have you to thank, in its richness through our large family and in the orientation toward the Essential, that helps me over these times. I wish very much that the children, who in the meantime again have really grown, would get to know you properly and would come closer to you. But I will not interfere more in the unforeseeable future, so as not to leave behind any obligations for anyone. For me it is a great comfort that Emmi so bravely stands by her husband in this difficult situation.

I hope that some news from Aunt Elisabeth[15] comes after all. I have had, you know, a really special relationship with her that was founded on the Italian experience. Although we were never there together, certainly we have in some way spoken about it most of the times when we saw each other. Her aesthetic educational foundations and forms went as far back as Great-Grandfather's time. They continued to have an effect on her as an inactive person.

14. Brother, killed in 1918.
15. Elisabeth von Hase, sister of Klaus Bonhoeffer's mother. She died in the air attack on Dresden.

Now, farewell, dear Papa and dear Mama. We want to gain new hope from these Easter days, hope that this year will bring external and spiritual peace. I embrace both of you as your thankful and fortunate

Klaus

P.S. Be sure to give my hearty Easter greeting to my brothers and sisters, nephews and nieces.

[Approved Letter]

[Lehrter Street 3]
Easter 1945

My dear children,

I will not live much longer, and I want now to say goodbye to you. This becomes very hard for me, for I love each of you so much and you have always given me only joy. Now I will no longer see how you grow up and become responsible human beings. But I am quite confident that you are traveling the right path at Mama's hand and then too will find advice and support from relatives and friends. Dear children, I have seen much and experienced even more. But, my fatherly experiences can no longer guide you. For that reason, I would like to tell you some more things that are important for your lives, even if much of it will become clear to you only later.

Above all, continue to stand fast by Mama in love, trust, gallantry, and care as long as God preserves her for you. Always think about whether you can make her happy in some way. One day, when you are big, I wish for you that you will stay as affectionately close to your mother as I have remained to my parents. You know, one really understands one's parents only when one is an adult oneself. I have asked Mama to stay with me until the end. They were difficult but magnificent months. They were focused on the Essential and sustained by the love and the strong heart of your mother. You will understand that only later.

Keep your brothers and sisters, too, close and ever closer together. That you are so different is still sometimes an occasion for a quarrel. Only when you are older will you be able to give yourselves that much more in return. A quarrel once in a while is not so bad. But don't carry it around with you. Think then of me and quickly and cheerfully shake hands with each other again. Help one another where you can. If one of you is sad or ill humored, look after him until he is cheerful again. Don't drift apart from one another; care for what brings you together. Play, sing, and dance with one another as we have done so often. Don't isolate yourselves with your friends when you can let your brothers and sisters take part. That also strengthens the friendship.

On my right hand I wear the ring with which Mama has made me happy. It is the sign that I belong to her and to you too. The signet ring on my left hand reminds of the family to which we belong, of our ancestors and descendants. It says, Hear the voice of the past; do not lose yourself arbitrarily in the transitory present; be true to the good character of your family and pass it on to your children and grandchildren. Dear children, understand this special obligation correctly now. The respect for the past and the responsibility in regard to the future give the correct attitude for life. Stand proudly by your family, from which such strengths grow.

Demand much from yourself and from your friends. Striving for recognition makes slaves of you if you cannot also do without it gracefully, and not everyone can manage that. Pay no heed to cheap applause.

Accept the people whom you meet otherwise just the way they are. Don't take exception right off to what is foreign or displeases you, and look on the good side. Then you are not only more just, but you preserve yourself from narrow-mindedness. In the garden grow many flowers. The tulip blooms beautifully but has no scent, and the rose has its thorns. An open eye, however, also rejoices in the inconspicuous greenery. In this way one discovers the mostly hidden agreeable sides of people when one tries to understand them. Whoever is occupied only with himself has no taste for this. But believe me, dear children, life unfolds itself for you in the small and the large sphere only when you think not only of yourself but also of the others, when you experience what they have to offer. Whoever clings only to his own voice while making music, or even wants to hear only himself, misses the whole. But whoever performs it properly also lives as well in the noble melting away of his own instrument into the other voices. If you pattern your life in this way, it will be filled completely with this wider spirit. What is important is not only to step in now and then and help out. That certainly gives a lot of pleasure. But whoever receives with heartfelt thanks often gives more. To do justice to people is a part of this, and as well, to take a well-meaning interest in them and never to be a spoilsport. From this spirit too arises quite naturally, as a form of social intercourse, the politeness that wins people for you. Cultivate it as a fine worldly-wise art of the heart. Whoever understands how to accept people of power and influence properly, without forfeiting anything of inner freedom, can thereby have a very good effect. It would be foolish to despise one's *savoir-vivre*. If it is not given to you, then freely and naturally hold yourself back. But that can wait a long while. Only because I will no longer be living then do I speak about this now.

I hope that circumstances will permit you the calm and a long time for each one of you to grow up spiritually and mentally in your own way, and for each of you to learn much more, so that one day you will share in the inexhaustible happiness of a vital education. But do not seek the value of education in the high achievements it enables you to attain but rather in the fact that it ennobles the human being through the inner freedom and dignity it imparts. It widens your horizon in time and space. The contact with the noble and the great refines the sense of decency, judgment, and feeling, and kindles the never-extinguishing enthusiasm that knows no meager everyday existence. In this way you will become kings! Then master yourselves too. Out of this power, develop your gifts into efficiency and excellence. Then when the time is kind to you, the human being and not only the achievement will be appreciated.

I would wish for you that as long as you are young, you hike really a lot in the country, and that you absorb it in every respect and with all your senses. While hiking, one has all the time necessary to abandon oneself completely to the countryside and to the impressions of human beings, villages, and the beautiful old cities. When then while hiking and singing songs together, the fantasy of our own days strays into past times, then there emerges inscrutably before you, lost in thought, the image of the beautiful German country in which our own being is found. Then turn toward the south. In the never-fulfilled, wistful desire for sunny clarity lies our strength and our destiny.

The times of horror, of destruction, and of dying, in which you, dear children, are growing up, demonstrate the transitoriness of everything earthly, for all the glory of the human being is like the flower of the grass. Under the impression of this experience, we lead our lives in the consciousness of its transitoriness. But here begins all the wisdom and piety that turns away from the transitory to the eternal. That is the blessing of this time. Do not only abandon yourself, then, to the pious sentiments such shocks evoke or that, in the haste and confusion of this world now and then burst forth out of a feeling of emptiness, but rather deepen and strengthen them. Do not remain in the twilight but rather struggle toward clarity without injuring the gentle and desecrating the Unapproachable. Get into the Bible and take for yourself possession of this world in which what matters most is what you have experienced and what you yourself have acquired in all honesty. Then your lives will be blessed and happy. Farewell! God keep you!

In true love, I embrace you,
Your Papa

[Secret Message][16]

[23 April 1945]

Dearest, I am now suddenly being transferred after all, and I want, nevertheless, to entrust this letter to you. Use it at the time that seems right to you. I must pack quickly.

I kiss you!

Your Klaus

16. In the cellar of the prison at Lehrter Street 3, on the night immediately before his murder. The letter mentioned has been lost.

HANS
VON DOHNANYI

Born 1 January 1902 in Vienna—after legal examinations, in the Documentation Department of the Foreign Office—1925, marriage to Christine Bonhoeffer; in the same year, named *Assistent*[1] at the Institute for Foreign Policy of the University of Hamburg—from 1929, personal assistant to the Reich justice minister—1938, Reich judicial councilor in Leipzig—end of August 1939, special chief on Canaris's[2] staff in charge of the political section—arrested 5 April 1943—executed 9 April 1945 in the concentration camp at Sachsenhausen.

Reminiscence

[To Ricarda Huch]

   I will now try to give a picture of my husband as I have it in my mind, in part from his reports, in part from our own experience to-

---

   1. [A position roughly comparable to that of instructor in an American university.]
   2. [Admiral Wilhelm Canaris was chief of the *Abwehr,* the German military intelligence and espionage service, and also a member of the resistance. He was executed at the Flossenbürg concentration camp on 9 April 1945.]

gether. We have known each other since he was seventeen and I was fifteen years old.

My husband spent his early childhood along with his one-year-younger sister (who later became the wife of my oldest brother) in Berlin-Grunewald, where his father had moved after he had become a professor at the Berlin Conservatory.

Until he was eleven years old, he and his sister must have had an untroubled, happy childhood. He said later that when he thought about his childhood, there appeared before him the garden at Knaus Street, his sister, the dogs, and, in bed before going to sleep in the evenings, the chamber music or piano playing of his parents which filtered up into the children's bedroom from the music room. Thus for years music simply belonged to the process of falling asleep for him, and still later when he just could not sleep—which, to be sure, did not occur often—the best method for him to fall asleep was to imagine a musical experience. So, music really always remained something highly personal for him, and his whole life long he preferred chamber music to the big Philharmonic concerts. His own ability, however, did not extend beyond the accompaniment of short children's songs. Although his mother—who, in this connection, was quite critical—considered him unusually musically gifted, his instruction was broken off after several short trials. Mother and son were, as both later admitted, too impatient. Both later quite often regretted it. Well prepared by what he had absorbed as a child, my husband retained a fine ear for tone, rhythm, and the dynamics of each work—many times to the great regret of both parties while our children were practicing—and a love for music, without which his life would have been unthinkable.

The image of his father was bound up for him with the memory of the days around Christmas, when this professionally very busy man had time only for his children. Then there was time to play, and to make music, with the children. Thus, my husband said, his father once played for him on the piano variations upon his favorite song, "Gestern abend ging ich aus . . ." [I went out last evening . . .], variations he always wanted so much to hear once again in his life. A friend who was a singer came and the children were allowed to pick out their favorite songs; my husband always chose the "Heinzelmännchen," by Löwe.[3] He said later that he no longer knew for sure whether he chose them because of their length or their mysterious air.

My husband often later asserted that his father had been, in spite of the cult the Berlin concert world at that time made out of him, basically a quite childlike, simple human being who had enjoyed his children in harmless joy and who had been separated, perhaps by his wife out of consideration for his artistic work, in an unnecessary and fateful way from them and from daily family life by a curtain impenetrable to the children.

His mother was a person who was unusually gifted artistically. There are musically competent people who preferred her piano playing to that of her husband—in any case, as far as chamber music and accompaniment are concerned. For my husband, her piano playing was the embodiment of what he loved in music. But she was also a difficult person who did not make life easy for her fellow human beings. My husband was devoted in tender love to her his entire life, although she also caused him many difficult hours through her lack of understanding for the work of a man and her almost jealous claims on his time.

When my husband was eleven years old, his parents separated. The children remained with their mother. Guilt and innocence are difficult to decide here. His father believed he had found the woman who gave him what he needed. His mother believed in a temporary straying, and only very late did she bury the hopes in her heart for his return.

In the eyes of the children, it was an unprepared, incomprehensible break. My husband said later that the love-starved heart of a child now wanted to love both parents equally at once, and that he regarded the conflict before which he now had been placed as quite awful. . . .

The father moved to the conservatory in Budapest—which led to a complete break in the relationship. . . . My husband in his mature years, when he himself was already a father of three children, took the step of restoring relations with his father, to the joy of both.

3. [Karl Löwe (1796–1869) was a composer of ballads. The ballad mentioned here is a long poem, set to music, about fairies and sprites.]

Through the separation of the parents, the economic circumstances of the family changed very suddenly. Up to this point, life had been secure and happy in the family's own house and garden, with many servants, a French maid, and much luxury that was advantageous to the children. Now the situation became very constrained. A new apartment was found; the mother gave music lessons and in the evenings played much chamber music. My husband, from the age of fourteen on, tutored students from the lower school classes. He continued this activity into the first semester of his study at the university. When he was nineteen years old, a job in the Foreign Office was offered to him upon the recommendation of Professor Hans Delbrück, whose son Justus had been his close friend since earliest childhood. I still recall how happy he was at that time to be able finally to earn his living in a way that did not mean a loss of time for him but, rather, a great joy.

Along with school and tutoring, he found time for intensive and, for a young man of his age, astonishingly systematic reading. His wish even then was to become a historian. Later there once came into my hands excerpts from Mommsen, Ranke, Meyer, and works of the philosophy of history and literary history which he had made for himself while reading in his last school years. Much diligence, much effort to get to the bottom of things, often naively overbearing criticism—but in any case, there was a great deal of seriousness in it. Unfortunately, they went the way of almost all his possessions in the days of struggle! School itself was an incidental thing for him. He was a good but not a model student; as a small boy, he played the usual devilish tricks; as a bigger boy, he felt a gradually emerging indifference. My husband and I became acquainted at school. At that time, the only possible path to a humanist education for girls in our area was to go to a boys' secondary school. When I entered the second form, my husband went into the top form.[4] That was in the summer of 1919.

From this point on, it becomes very hard for me to write to you . . .

---

4. [The German school system then, as now in some areas, employed a grade system common to most European countries. Thus, the terms *Obersekunda* and *Oberprima* have been translated, in a sense common to British secondary schools, as "second form" and "top form."]

about the things that lie deepest in my heart. . . . But I must speak about them because they have become a part of those things concerning him and myself without which one can neither perceive nor understand the character of my husband.

In the *Forsyte Saga*, by Galsworthy, there are some very beautiful words about what can emerge for the mature human being from a youthful love. From this at first innocent affection and friendship the fulfillment of both our lives developed. It is certainly rare that friendship and love are brought into our hearts in the form of one and the same human being. We ourselves stood during our lives together with astonished thankfulness before this gift from God and remained friends and lovers of each other.

When my husband was twenty-three and I was twenty-one years old, we married.[5] We then, as was jokingly said in the family, always had our examinations at the same time. Three days after the birth of our daughter, my husband had his doctoral examination; during my confinement with our eldest son, he had his assessor's examination. We had little money, a great deal of work, and were very happy. I worked with him night after night; that is, I typed his papers, discussed and disputed with him about his judgments and papers, and attempted to relieve him of as much work as I could, for up to his assessor's examination, he had, of course, to attend to his university work along with his court practice. So the nights often had to be

5. In a second letter to Ricarda Huch, Christine von Dohnanyi wrote the following additional reminiscences of the first years of their marriage:

About our time in Hamburg, it can be said that we married there and spent the first years of our marriage there. My husband at that time performed his service as a junior lawyer in the city administration there and, at the same time, was an *Assistent* at the Institute for Foreign Policy. Given what Hamburg meant as a city of the Hanse and as an overseas trading center, we had less direct contact—unless one wants to count my husband's passion for harbor tours and for observing the steamers sailing in and out, a passion about which I often teased him. But in the end, the whole spirit of the Hamburg administration had an air of cosmopolitanism, and my husband enjoyed the broad-mindedness in the Hamburg judicial service, with which even a minor judge approached problems, and always understood it as an effect of this rather international feeling. The *Bürgermeister* at that time, Petersen, thought very highly of my husband and always encouraged him in a friendly way in his interests and desires. Later, when he was in the Central Office in Berlin, the friendly ties to many a civil servant in the Hamburg administration and judicial service continued to exist.

sacrificed. His whole life long he had a quite unusual capacity for work and certainly, also, very good health. Otherwise, he could not have achieved what he had to at that time. In the process, he gave no consideration to his physical well-being. He suffered, for example, from severe migraines but did not like it at all when I took notice of it or even wanted to get him to take something for it. He considered seeking compensation for too short a night by sleeping longer the next morning to be a "weakness." He was of the opinion that each day had its own twenty-four hours, and when one wanted to carry a minus from the day before over into the next day, then, in the end, there was nothing more left for a person. At the same time, he could be tremendously lazy during his vacation days. He could lie many hours on the meadow and doze and daydream, play with the children, or make toys for them with an almost childlike enthusiasm. He did not then like at all to make any kind of plans for the day; he didn't even want a walk to be scheduled beforehand. At the end of the vacation there also came regularly that morning-after feeling. With the benefit of more and more experience, I myself then always called his attention in the last vacation days to the fact that this feeling now certainly would come soon. Of the books to which he had been looking forward the entire year and of the work he had intended to do during the vacation, only half was completed. The letters he wanted to write were never written. There was self-reproach about the lost time, poor organization of time, his own lack of energy—I could, after all, easily predict all of it and accepted both, laziness and the morning-after feeling, as a necessity. They formed the few hours of compensation for a constantly overstrained capacity for work.

There certainly are human beings who are always burdened to the limits of their strength. My husband was one of them. Until his assessor's examination, it was his double profession that hardly left him time for himself; later it was the responsible positions, unusual for his years, that he as personal assistant to the minister assumed in the Ministry. Up to 1933, he had the wish to qualify as a university lecturer in constitutional and international law. He had completed the preparatory work for a treatise about the legal status of the political party in the state. During the National Socialist period, outlines and card files about this treatise were banished to the attic. After the confiscation of our house for Russian troops, I found the individual slips of paper scattered about the house, ripped apart, soiled, and torn up.

From 1933 on, it was other things that claimed his every free hour and that gave him inner comfort, and many times satisfaction, too, and led him along the way he then went.

I want to try to report to you about these things some other time. I too went all of these ways together with him. Our life together, simply of its own accord, excluded the possibility of secrets kept from each other. It was a matter of course that he told these things and discussed them with me, just as it was a matter of course that I kept quiet about them. I even think that he never would have gone this way if I had opposed him, but it was also precisely a result of our togetherness that I never could have hindered him in this path in which he saw his task and which became our common fate.

Whoever did not know my husband fairly well saw in him at first the reserved, certainly unusually intelligent and helpful, administrative civil servant. The letters I receive today from his closer co-workers and friends all speak nostalgically of the amiable cheerfulness and the superior humor with which he dealt with things. In fact, among my dearest memories is how much we laughed with each other. I think often that it is indeed perhaps the sign of the deepest mutuality when one can laugh with each other about the same things. He had a great instinct for a good joke; toward the jokes of a certain category usual in officers' circles, however, he had an almost overly sensitive aversion that brought upon him many a gibe. In general, he had the impression that he, as decidedly a civilian in the OKW,[6] enjoyed a certain "fool's freedom," of which he made abundant use in the form of great openness in the criticism of his superiors and their actions.

The love for nature and animals remained with my husband his entire life. With dogs he had quite a unique relationship that was passed down to one of our children. There was no nasty and vicious dog with which my husband would not have played calmly from the

6. [*Oberkommando der Wehrmacht*, or General Staff of the German *Wehrmacht*.]

first moment on. I was once witness to a scene where Admiral Canaris, who also was crazy about dogs, declared to my husband proudly that his dog did not go to any stranger. My husband laughed and said, "That would indeed be the first dog . . . ," slapped his thighs, and before he knew it the dog was sitting in his lap to the dismayed astonishment of Canaris. A bird fallen from its nest, a newborn kid, a sick rabbit could tear my husband away from the most responsible work, and then they occupied him a while to the exclusion of everything else.

With the exception of a brief period of the most severe lack of housing, we always lived at the edge of the city in open country, and my husband, in times of his heaviest work loads and when he did not yet have a car, took upon himself the long way rather than to live in the city. I believe he gathered a great deal of strength from the tranquillity in nature, and I really have never seen another human being enjoy the peace of an evening in the country with such joy and so passionately as he did.

In prison he certainly suffered at first almost as much from the separation from all of nature as from the separation from the children and me. His letters from this period demonstrate this.

On walks he often had said, while considering some picturesquely exciting view, "I would like to be able to paint that." Into the loneliness of his confinement I sent him pastels and pencils. He then, partly from memory, partly with the aid of photographs, made sketches of our children, and later of himself too, that amazed various artists to whom I showed them later. None of them wanted to believe me when I said that this man had never before in his life learned to draw. This seems to me to be something similar to the poems of my brother Dietrich Bonhoeffer. Constantly being alone certainly brings much that is latent to unexpected bloom. . . .

I have told you here about my husband as simply as I am able. It is not easy, and whether it can give you a picture of him, I do not dare judge. He was not an average person; everyone who knew him knows that. And so it is hard to place things in correct proportion in their relationship to one another. . . .

Christine von Dohnanyi

[Christine von Dohnanyi to Barbara, Klaus, and Christoph. Approved
Letter]

[Charlottenburg Women's Prison]

Easter Sunday, 25 April 1943

My beloved children,

Today is Easter Sunday, and so I too must speak with you a little bit
for once. Actually, I can write a letter twice a week now, but Father is
completely alone and so I always write to him and have asked him to
write to you. So all of you get the news, even if infrequently. Since I
have been here, I have received a letter from Bärbel and one from
Grandfather and one from Father. But, you should know that I am
healthy and that my thoughts are always with you, and in addition, I
have time, time like never before in my life, to be alone with my
thoughts. Just think, Chris, in the space of three weeks I have spoken
all in all perhaps three to four hours with other people! How would you
like that? I read a lot and am thankful for every book, and then, of
course, I also go for walks, always nicely back and forth in the cell by
the open window. I eat from a nice white enameled bowl such as I
never had at home. Then I sleep as often as possible, and in the after-
noons when it does not happen to be a holiday, I go for a walk for half
or three-quarters of an hour in a yard from which one can see, in any
event, only the sky. So that's what my life looks like. And just think: I
never search for anything now when I have so much time that I would
find it really nice to search properly for my purse or the keys for once.
Everything is always immediately at hand, for it lies either on the table
or in the suitcase. I would like to introduce this at home too. And in
general, one sees how good it is when one has few needs. Remember
that. Not for the jail but for your life.

You know as much as I do about why I am sitting here, but don't
take it tragically. However and whenever, one day everything must be
cleared up, and then they'll certainly let me come home too. So don't
be sad but rather be happy and enjoy every beautiful moment. Don't
think, Now we make merry and have our fun, although our parents are
locked up. On the contrary, precisely because it is our only joy and
comfort that you are happy, you should be cheerful out of love for us.

And then don't be embarrassed, and don't let anyone give you a dumb look. Always calmly carry your head just a little bit higher, and then the people by themselves will stop doing that. How much I would like to stand by you in this time, because I know how hard it is for you all. But that does not lie in my power. Do your work with much diligence, and remember that you make me happy with it. You, my little Chris, practice diligently and seriously. Everything that all of you still can learn now, learn it. And be orderly with your things, and frugal. I also would like to know how your existence will develop now after the vacation. But I don't want to interfere from this distance. You must discuss it with your grandparents and Aunt Ursel. Perhaps I can talk to Aunt Ursel about it, and I will also request that you be permitted to visit me. You are, indeed, old enough not to make a big tragedy out of it, and it really would be nice to see each other once.

Now I want to tell you one more thing: Don't carry any hate in your heart against the power that has done this to us. Don't fill your young souls with bitterness; that has its revenge and takes from you the most beautiful thing there is, trust. We have, you know, never spoken much with each other about religious things. Not everyone can speak about these things. But I want to say to you that I am so convinced that all things work together for good to those who love God—and our entire life has proved it again and again—that, in all the loneliness and worry about all of you, I was really never in despair even for a moment. You probably will be surprised that I am saying this about a subject toward which you no doubt have believed that I have a great reserve. In my case, it is just that I must already be sitting in prison to be able to express something like this, and perhaps also to be able to comfort you by saying that I do not suffer as much as you probably think. Read the text we wrote for you in your Bible, Barbie.

And then, one more thing. Use your gifts and, thinking of us, try to come to terms with life independently. The future is dark for everyone, certainly, but to a special degree for us at the moment. We have given to you what we could; show that we have done it properly. Be diligent and modest, not self-opinionated but independent, helpful, and obedient. Then you will be liked and will be able to be of use everywhere. Stand by one another, help one another, and speak to each other when one of you does something that would not please us. And when it comes from one another, listen to it as though it came from us.

I cannot write an extra letter to your grandparents, who I would so much like to thank here for all their care. I can't let Father go long without news. Give them a kiss from me and tell them that I still hope to see them in good health again soon. Here sit all kinds of people without any family. To sit in jail without all the cares for one's loved ones must be a real pleasure. It is hardest of all to deal with this.

Now it will no doubt soon be six, when the baby gets her supper. By the way, always so abundantly that I can't eat a third of it. Then comes quite a long evening, because there isn't any light. But it too passes. Now greet your grandparents, Aunt Ursel, and Uncle Rüdiger, and thank them a thousand times. Also greet all the other aunts and uncles. Farewell; I give each of you a kiss. Believe me, when one has experienced this, then one knows that it is after all only a really small and meager part of the human being that one can put in jail. I embrace all of you.

Your Mama

Klaus, my big boy, will you take my place in the garden?

[Approved Letter to his wife]

[Prinz Albrecht Street 8]
8 February 1945

Beloved, I have been here for a week. I am well; please, please don't worry! The bunker is holding.[7] And don't come into the city on my account! I received your packages of 23 and 30 January yesterday. I hope the letters too were not burned up. I don't know anything about you all, but I carry your little picture on my breast, and you and the children in my heart. Thus do I deal with this situation too, in hope and in faith. Write to me, my angel, about how you are, what the children

---

7. On 3 February 1945, the heaviest daylight attack on Berlin took place, which also heavily damaged the buildings of Prinz Albrecht Street.

are doing, what news there is from little Klaus.[8] Yesterday, it was said that my daughter (Maria?)[9] had been here, that she would come again this week. But obviously nothing was delivered. Unfortunately, I was not successful in getting the information through that I have laundry to exchange (dirty and torn). If possible, add: comb, extra glasses, candle, underwear, shoes, [the end of the sentence made unreadable with ink by the censor]. Thanks so much for all the beautiful things you have sent me. The cigarettes were greatly welcome! On the twelfth,[10] I will be with you, you my all, in all my thoughts, desire, love, and thankfulness for the life you make worth living for me anew every day!

Your Husband. Kiss the children.

Only now do I discover this space that is still blank. So I can still write my kiss for you here. The things you sent are all still quite edible and I am now abundantly supplied. Please, if at all possible, matches, some money, and six-, eight-, and twelve-pfennig stamps. But I am counting on the fact that no one, above all, not you, will risk the dangers of an alarm on my account! Whoever comes here might, in any case, wait for the laundry I have to exchange. Warm things are now the best. I kiss your hand, my darling. Greetings to all!

Hans

[Approved Letter]

[Prinz Albrecht Street 8]
On our twentieth anniversary
12 February 1945

My dearly beloved darling,
  I hope that my card from last week reached you. Now, when everything else must take a back seat to the great general distress, I am happy, and all of you will be glad about every tiny sign of life. The

8. Son Klaus.
9. Maria von Wedemeyer, the fiancée of Dietrich Bonhoeffer.
10. Wedding day.

letter from little Klaus of 28 January—up to now the only one—was such a joy! On Friday (9 February), another package from you was brought down to me, probably from 7 February. A letter was not with it, but your letters of 23 and 30 January were. But I will have patience even now when it is especially hard for me. I don't know how all of you withstood the attack, but I am so glad that you didn't worry a great deal about me, and you don't need to. What I would like to say to you today would be only for us two alone. The happiness you give me anew every day—for twenty years now—and the certainty of your great love are the whole content of my life and fill every hour of my existence. How poor most people are! Stay for me from one day to the next what you are for me: my happiness, my pride! If, in spite of everything, I could only be by your side in this difficult time! The war probably will scatter the family too now. But how many today have to leave house and home and hardly know where to go! I am so sorry for Aunt Elisabeth! I definitely had hoped that she would be here; nevertheless, I am glad that she found a refuge in time. Who is helping you now around the house? I suppose you will use the lower corridor as living quarters for refugees. One must help where one can; but let yourself too be helped! Don't worry about me! The great misery of the people outside makes one's own fate appear irrelevant. My health is essentially the same as it was. [There follows here a sentence made unreadable by the censor with ink.] Write to me about how you are, what the children, especially Klaus, are doing. I hope you are not angry about my wishes. I need underwear badly; if possible, colored [following sentence made unreadable by the censor with ink], also handkerchiefs are very much desired. But, you surely know, don't you, that all this stands under the heading "All of you come first!" In Klaus's letter, it says, "Food better than at home!" That worries me. In my pantry now is a lot of butter, bread, sausage. You must now, after the cutbacks in rationing, really think a bit more about yourselves. You and the children must stay healthy, and I should not eat up so much of your food. Whoever of you comes here with things for me might—merely for the sake of your convenience—please not go away but rather just wait for the laundry to be exchanged, which I keep ready. I am taking pains with my handwriting; it is dusk and your package (as support)

wobbles. Outside, it appears about ready to snow—you will have difficulties with transportation here again. Please stay at home! Don't think
you have to bring me something often. I would rather know that you
are safe than to have something for myself that—a sign of the times—
so many must do without. I think I will write to you soon with a little
something for little Klaus added on, so that he receives an answer from
me after all; just as soon as writing day is here again. How beautiful
this day was twenty years ago! And the fourteen days of fritters and
kidney soup; I would like so much to have them made again by your
dear hand! God preserve you and the children, my angel! I think only
of you!

Your husband

[Approved Letter]

[Prinz Albrecht Street 8]
18 February 1945

My most dearly beloved darling,
The letter from our wedding anniversary reached you, I hope. It was
a somewhat prosaic letter, but that was due to the required shortness.
The new style still requires a lot of effort from me! From you, since 30
January, no letter, but yesterday a second one from Klaus. The boy is
not going to the dogs; we don't have to worry at all about that! I have
made up my mind to attach a letter to him today. But before I forget it:
at one time, *Standartenführer*[11] Huppenkothen was so friendly as to
bring my glasses with him to me in Sachsenhausen. But unfortunately,
they have by mistake wandered back. I am somewhat angry about my
eyes: without glasses they don't want to work correctly. Please send
me the spare glasses (−3 both sides) after all; they are probably lying
well ordered in the box marked "Glasses." But you surely know: I
would rather wait a little bit longer than that you drive in from Sackrow

11. [The organization of the SA and SS included regimental-sized units called *Stan-
darten*. The commanders of these units were *Standartenführer*, or colonels. Smaller
units, below battalion size, were commanded by *Untersturmführer*, or second lieuten-
ants; cf. p. 63.]

only because of the glasses. Please don't do it! Promise me! I am depending on you! That you run the risk of an alarm once a week and make such an effort on my account torments me enough as it is! Klaus's help was such a comfort! You receive letters from him often—that makes me happy! How thankful one must be when one can just simply write letters to one's loved ones so often and so much about what's on one's mind! But how many "obvious" things of this kind there really are whose value I have become aware of only through the bitter experience of doing without them! Really, the human being lives not only from bread alone! Apropos, some money please; I must pay for a newspaper and two cigarettes everyday; also stamps. And now a kiss for the children. Klaus and his "letter" should not come up too short. Day and night I think of nothing more than you and the children. My heart and my soul—I left them both with all of you! . . .

Your husband

My dear boy, I am so happy about your letters, and I would like to write you at least a little bit here. I hope very much that we will see each other very soon and will be able to speak about so many different things. I know you well enough not to worry about you. Just stay yourself and keep your faith, your fatherland, and your home as your sources of strength. Nothing has brought me so close to you as has your care for your mother. You are beginning to sense now what she is to me, what she is to all of you. In everything you do and when you are at loggerheads with yourself, think of her; then you will not lack for advice, the purity of your soul will not run into danger, and what may be sacred to the man in you will not be profaned. Pray to God for a simple heart, and try to accept gladly and with thanks what fate brings you. I am pleased that all of you have a portion of the inner serenity that reduces things to their proper size, a gift of your mother, whom I love so much because there is nothing so liberating and superior as a laugh where the others are able to perceive only the unpleasantness of life. I wish you much of this strength, through which we learn with a smile to adapt. Yearnings remain—of course! Looking at the stars with Mama and all of you, sitting by the sea and chatting, breathing the air of the forest—how clearly I remember all of that! And also passing the bottle around in merry company—but come, why imagine such things? They will come again. I hold to the wonderful verse you have written for me (I didn't know it) and I hold to the fact that our thoughts often meet, my good dear little fellow, you! Don't worry about me; I am doing well. That you do a good job is, for us, a matter of course, but I am still a bit proud of you! God keep you, my boy, you, your beloved mother, your brother and sister. We will stay together!

Your faithful Father

23 February 1945

The sending of my letter has been delayed somewhat. A thousand thanks for the package from the day before yesterday. Everything had to go so fast that I didn't get to have transmitted to you the few requests I have.

One thing I may mention: *money* received. When there is a chance, please think again about the *glasses;* perhaps they are in the coat I had in the military hospital. During the alarms, I always stuck them in one of the inner pockets. In any case, -3 diopter on both sides; perhaps something similar (-2, for example, is better than nothing) is available in the family. *Pencils, eraser, magnifying glass* probably were left behind inadvertently in the little suitcase. I would appreciate very much: warm undershirt (have only the one on my back), warm long underwear, socks (if you can spare them), something to read, matches, nail clippers.

Deliver your *letters* here to the house prison; from here they are then directed to the censor by Detective Superintendent Sonderegger, who is responsible for me now. Then you have only half as much running around. You can also, of course, send letters with the post.

I have asked Mr. Sonderegger regarding the *preserving jars* [here two lines are erased] and will ask him to approve the delivery; it is indeed so difficult for you otherwise. But *please* think about yourselves in regard to food. I am really well supplied. I am doing well. How nice that little Klaus was at home for a day.

Kiss, Hans

[Secret Message from Prinz Albrecht Street, hidden in the bottom of a paper cup]

25 February [1945]

Dearest . . . , we have not seen each other now for half a year. My ardent wish: to see you! It is a dreadful time, and the fact that I cannot stand by your side and that of the children now is a torture in itself.

1. A few things for the others: I am informed about Lehrter Street 3[12] and what has occurred there up to three days ago.

I live only in my thoughts of all of you—you know that—and would like to help carry all of you. If I could only load everything on my shoulders! Perhaps the following is important for you: the director of Lehrter 3 is *Untersturmführer* Knuth. *Exceedingly decent,* has a soft spot for his prisoners, angling for an anchor for the future. Also the personnel in the office are good. If Ursel and Emmi want to see their husbands, they should express their wish in the office; it will be made possible if it in any way can be done. Mrs. Perels[13] saw him about five days ago.

2. Three days ago, a general practitioner from Berlin-Tempelhof who is also a prisoner (Dr. Eugen Ense,[14] Tempelhof, Löwenhardt Street 63) was ordered to take care of me. If anyone comes from him (daughter fifteen, son sixteen and a half years old), it is OK. Of course, I will send only a *personal* word. And please, vice versa. *Please, please* don't run any danger; the situation is critical enough.

Up until three days ago, I was given over to a caseworker who left nothing to be desired in the way of brutality.[15] He thought he could break me simply by letting me rot without any personal care at all. That went on for three weeks. But I just let myself stink. That helped. Then came Sonderegger and Ense, who can freely come and go in my cell (the door to my cell is open), and the roughest part was overcome. It was really only funny, and I have often laughed about how I looked.

---

12. Klaus Bonhoeffer and Rüdiger Schleicher had been condemned to death there on 2 February.
13. Friedrich Justus Perels likewise had received a death sentence on 2 February.
14. Prisoner at Lehrter Street 3.
15. Detective Superintendent Stawitzki.

As far as *my health* goes, it did *not* affect me. You know that I don't try to fool you! So I am counting on you that you will not worry about this. I am using my illness as a weapon. In the process, the fact that I am considered to be sicker than I really am is useful to me. Ense is of the opinion that I belong in a hospital and that my condition will continue to worsen because of the outward circumstances. That is, of course, not authoritative because Ense is, after all, a prisoner, but Sonderegger asks him and has let himself be influenced. In reality, I feel *well*, have really a lot of food now because of you. At night, I secretly teach myself how to walk. It's working out quite well (after all, I must see to it that I become able to rely on myself); days, I am the helpless sick person.

3. *Gaining time* is the *only* solution. I must see to it that I become unable to be interrogated. It would be best if I could get a respectable *dysentery*. A culture for medical purposes ought to be available in the Koch Institute. If you put a red cover on a container of food—an ink spot on the container too would be best—then I'll know that a decent infection, which will bring me into the hospital, is in it. I am not afraid of *any* illness; am convinced that I will see it through. It can, of course, happen that I will not respond to the bacillus; then that's just the way it is.

4. One now desires to conclude the affair violently, and that must be prevented. Up to now, I have been left almost completely alone because I had told Huppenkothen already on 24 August that they ought not take any pains with me; I wouldn't name any names.

Now, says Sonderegger, I couldn't incriminate anyone, everything is known. Besides that, other sirens can be heard: he says it's desired that I be taken to a hospital so that I become healthy, that there is no interest in putting me before the People's Tribunal, that there is respect for my conduct, etc. *Everything* a lie! In any case, *this* is the assumption on which we must *always* primarily proceed! I fear that others have been taken in by such things. On the other hand, Sonderegger has said that if I did not give in now, he possibly would come into difficulties in regard to the "liability of the family" (by which he meant to threaten me with your arrest). But I myself believe that he would *not* do that willingly. And it must *under no circumstances* come to that!!! Sonderegger loves it when one lays particular stress on the gentleman in him, and he is not without a heart (but cunning). He vehemently criticizes Roeder's[16] methods of investigation.

5. Between us it is clear and also corresponds to the truth (1) that I have never let you in on official things, or such things with which I am charged, and (2) that I have *never* sent secret messages out to you. In case of emergency, you know only of an *attempt* to deliver a *love letter* to you with the laundry, which Maas[17] discovered and about which I told you later in the Charité. We have also not talked about my legal proceedings (too disgusting). Sonderegger does *not* have any interest in the old proceedings. He says he has always advocated the point of view that one ought not to frame a man like me if one cannot bag him otherwise.

6. I hope that postal connections are better now. In any case, *please:*

1. Always write a greeting and a short message on the list of contents (permissible).
2. Write on the wrapping paper: Greetings from Christel, Bärbel, Chris; then I know who is at home.
3. An exclamation mark after such a greeting means: message is inside (e.g., stuff it in the tip of a homemade cigarette or in a nut).
4. Also, three of you could write the list of contents, so that I know you are healthy and together.
5. Colored handkerchief means: everything OK with us. (Chris brought me one on Friday, to my great joy.)
6. *Always*, even when you come unexpectedly, have someone ask whether I might have something to send along or to ask for. And you yourself send word about how you are doing. By demanding the return of the packaging material (bag, etc.), one forces the people to deliver the message.
7. If Police Sergeant *Runge* is here, rely on him.
8. Coat, boots, socks, underwear, glasses (tendency: I must be prepared for all emergencies, Russians, etc.), also some more money.

---

16. Supreme Military Court Counselor Roeder, the chief interrogator from 1943.
17. Lieutenant Colonel Maas, the commandant of the Military Prison, Lehrter Street 61.

7. Felix—Call—Palace Hotel.[18] I will look for all of you, in any case, at home first of all. Possibly message under rock at the bridge.

Think about keeping my letters from the KZ[19] with no. 93033 as identification for all of you.

For Klaus, recommendation Havemann.[20]

According to previous experience, Russians make house searches most of the time at night. In case of danger, don't be at home nights.

The parents should move in with us. The *Heerstrasse*[21] certainly will be fiercely defended. If you think it is right, bury foodstuffs and valuables. I consider famine inevitable. I still have a *lot* of grape sugar.

9 [*sic*]. When you receive this, please put *toothpaste* in the package. Please, please do not put yourself in danger. If possible, do not drive into the city. I prefer to know that you are in Sackrow. Think about the matter of the production of a new infection. Zutt[22] perhaps will be able to make such a dish for you. It ought not to be too far in the future, because otherwise I may be taken out of Berlin. Wrap infected food in red *and* a sign on the container; if the idea cannot be realized, put *green* paper over any kind of food. If I go to a hospital in Berlin, then practically only State Hospital comes into consideration. I have briefly made mention of Zinn (Babelsberg). A dumb inquiry from a doctor (Papa, de Crinis?),[23] of Huppenkothen (who is Sonderegger's superior), whether care and *treatment* (passive exercises, massage, injections) are possible here would possibly also be helpful. Do *not* intervene yourself!

My darling! I have written you regularly. The letters have not been given to you; there were sketches of you with them. I still have here

---

18. Not explained.

19. [*Konzentrationslager* = concentration camp.]

20. The physicist Robert Havemann, a friend of Karl-Friedrich Bonhoeffer.

21. [The house of the Bonhoeffer parents was located on the Marienburger Allee, a street only a short distance from the Heerstrasse. The latter was, and is (primarily in West Berlin), a long, straight, broad avenue running straight through the center of Berlin and originally so laid out to facilitate the movements of military units; thus the street had the name Army Street.]

22. Professor Jürg Zutt, student and colleague of Professor Karl Bonhoeffer who often stayed at Sackrow because of the frequent air-raid alarms.

23. Professor Max de Crinis, successor in the academic chair of Professor Karl Bonhoeffer; at the same time, SS leader. On his role in the legal proceedings against Hans von Dohnanyi, see E. Bethge, *Dietrich Bonhoeffer*, 907–8.

what I had for you for 12 February. I love you so tremendously much, have such a great yearning, live only in you, for you! You know that.

Kisses! Hans

27 February

Good morning, my darling. . . . If all I needed to do was just to stretch out my hand to caress your head, a firm kiss, a glance at the lake, and out of the bed! I love you so madly. You really must not worry on account of me. I wanted to tell you: the bunker here is holding. On 3 February, the building received no fewer than eight direct hits, and in the bunker we shook only a little bit. It didn't even get any cracks. Then: the containers, I think, are very well suited for messages. Only, the bottom must be entirely *smooth* and must fit tightly all the way around. When there is a greeting with an exclamation mark on the container—you can also simply *underline* the greeting—I will search for a message in it. *Please, please* do *not* send me any infected food when there is a danger of infection for you in doing so! You must not get sick! Huppenkothen is Sonderegger's superior. Avoid a Detective Superintendent Stawitzki. Stawitzki was up to now a caseworker (*his* superior, too, is Huppenkothen). I tell Dr. Ense so much about our life. You have made everything like a wonderful dream for me. Again and again I end up talking about you! . . .

I must say one more thing: Runge has a *soft spot* for Maria. You may have heard his name through her (which she must know about). He also found Dietrich to be a "decent human being." Perhaps if she goes about it cleverly, he will tell her where Dietrich has got to. Your greetings and short message on the list of contents from last week, which Anna[24] brought, have made me so awfully happy—the first "letter" from you since 30 January. Such short messages are permissible. Always write me something on the list of contents, OK? I would like to know what you and the children are doing, how it is going with your

---

24. The Schleichers' maid.

civilian duties. The hardest thing for me is that I am dependent only on my fantasy. But write letters too! Please! . . . That's the way it is; one just can't stop! So much still comes to my mind, and I would like to express to you so much love. Don't be angry that I have wishes that are so hard to fulfill. I hear, for example, that outside there are no more *matches;* that is something I didn't know! Don't trouble yourself. Please send me a lighter. Perhaps I can get fluid here. Regarding the jars, appeal to the fact that up to now I always received some; if necessary, they can be delivered to the kitchen (that is the regulation). Please write what all of you are doing. I don't know anything about each of you in particular. If you have written or delivered a letter, *underline* my name on the list of contents. I have cell 28. Runge is on duty on Wednesday, 7 March, then always every other day. I saw Dietrich; he looked chipper. . . .

If I should leave here, then date without indication of place means: I have been taken away. Place then emerges from the beginning letters of words number 1, 3, 2, 4 in the corresponding lines. . . .

Send me a pair of gloves if you have got them. Kiss the children. What is going on in regard to their mobilization? Will Klaus come home once more before his induction into the *Wehrmacht?* I estimate eight to ten weeks yet, then the war will be over. After the fall of Stettin, an offensive against Berlin. Take care of yourself, my darling!

Kisses! Hans

[Approved Letter]

Berlin
[Prinz Albrecht Street 8]
8 March 1945

My beloved darling,

Thank you so much for the beautiful things you again sent me yesterday. The warm coffee was so relaxing—how long it has been since I have enjoyed something as good! I don't want to be unreasonable, but if you can enclose a little thermos for me now and then, that would be wonderful. Brewing coffee is almost too good for here. The bonbons too were quite timely. I have a bit of scratchiness in the throat—nothing special, certainly will pass soon—so it is good to have something to suck on. Do you have some more of them? I hope the drawings, which were kindly handed over to the children through Mr. Sonderegger, were a small joy for you. Because of all the coming and going, the dust, etc., Barbie's picture probably was smeared quite a bit, and I would be sorry about that, above all for the watercolor. In the meantime, the garden has indeed changed quite a bit, and I also realize that the groups of trees are spread out somewhat too much. I have shown them this way intentionally, in order to make the view of the house freer—"artistic freedoms." Little Klaus's picture must be postponed. The lighting conditions here are different from Sachsenhausen and unfortunately my right arm is bothering me again—but it is nothing serious. Mr. Sonderegger read me your letter of 27 February; there has been an objection to a sentence in it. Please do ask when you have a chance which one it is, so that you can act accordingly. I am so happy that there is good news from little Klaus. I hope he has also got my letter by now. What about his *Abitur?* Has he received it? On this matter, I believe, a special resolution of the teaching staff is required. In the *Völkischen Beobachter*[25] from 2 March, there was a report, and according to it, school instruction in Potsdam is now supposed to occur by means of homework assignments and communal instruction at home. Is Chris affected by this? Barbie's progress in learning to be an interpreter (where is the school anyway?) would interest me very much. Yesterday was Grete's[26] birthday—I wonder how they might have celebrated it. Karl-Friedrich will hardly have driven in. The pages are always so small! But the space is big enough still for a kiss for the children; I press you firmly to my heart!

Your husband

25. [After 1919, a pre–World War I weekly gossip sheet from Munich was renamed the *Völkischer Beobachter* and acquired by the fledgling NSDAP. Hitler, as head of the party, took control of it in 1921. His chief editor from 1923 was Alred Rosenberg. Until the collapse of the Third Reich in 1945, the daily *Völkischer Beobachter* was the official newspaper of the party and purveyor of its political and racial opinions.]

26. Grete, who was his sister and the wife of Karl-Friedrich Bonhoeffer, was with the children at Friedrichsbrunn.

[Secret Message from Prinz Albrecht Street]

Thursday, 8 March

My most dearly beloved darling,

   You can hardly imagine with what a pounding heart I saw a red-covered container emerge from the small suitcase yesterday. Then the book and—somewhat too hastily opened up—the thermos bottle! Finally, finally, a few lines from you—since more than half a year—a gift for which I have thanked the dear Lord in my nightly prayers. Thank you so very much, my love. Also, that you have delivered the letter (name underlined on the list of contents) and written the list of contents with the children and written the most important news on it! Runge grinned from ear to ear and said, "Maria is along, too." I hope he was able to say something to her about Dietrich. By the way, before I forget: In letters, if possible, do *not* write the name Sonderegger, because the letters can land in the hands of higher authorities and Sonderegger does not want to come under suspicion of granting us any kind of preferential treatment. He is flattered enough by the fact that I have mentioned him now several times in letters which I could hand over to him *directly*. The interrogations continue, and it is clear with what I have to reckon if a miracle doesn't happen.

   The misery around me is so great that I would throw away this little bit of life if *all of you* did not exist. But the thought of all of you, your great love, and my love for you gives me a will to live that is so strong that many times I believe it must prevail—and even if the world were filled with devils! (Or do you think only someone who possessed freedom could put that into poetry?) For that reason, I also do not fear *any* infectious disease. I know for sure that I would lie down with the feeling that this is the deliverance not only of my life but also of the lives of many others whose cause is bound up with mine—in any case, of Dietrich's. For all I care, cholera or typhus; of course, I stuck the diphtheria swab in my mouth immediately and chewed it up thoroughly, but for technical reasons it was not possible until 7:30 in the evening (Ense sat by my bed the whole time) and I had the feeling that the cotton already had become quite dry. Now I am eating up the bonbons as fast as I can. Diphtheria bacilli, as far as I understand, are not very volatile but cannot tolerate drying out but rather need a certain moisture to maintain themselves. Incubation period three to eight days. I *fear* that I am immune and will get nothing. But a repeat lies entirely in the realm of the possible. Send me a culture again at your leisure and *if you have something else too, then that in addition.* But make sure you watch out for yourself so that you do not catch something in the process!! Therefore, be careful too with the colored handkerchief; it may be, of course, that I now have become a carrier of the bacillus without becoming sick myself.

I *must* get out of here and into a hospital, *but in such a way* that I *cannot* be interrogated *further!* Bouts of unconsciousness and heart attacks command no respect, and if I go to the hospital *without* a new illness, that is even dangerous because then they will quickly make me well. Sonderegger said today, "It is in your own interests that the interrogations can be concluded soon. The *Reichsführer*[27] is not interested in keeping you here; he would like you to get well." Should I translate that? It means, "The *Reichsführer* would like to conclude the interrogations as soon as possible. In the period in which the bill of indictment is drafted, you are then to be brought to a hospital— perhaps to central Germany or to Bavaria (that depends entirely on the war situation). There we will sure enough make you fit for trial. One can hardly put you on trial in the condition you are in now, but in three to four weeks we'll have you ready!" I would so very much like to ruin these plans for these guys. Believe me—up to now I really have seen things correctly, *unfortunately; there is no solution other than a new serious illness.* Don't worry about me because of this! I will survive it. But even if that should not be the case, then much would be gained for the others, and for me—in effect—nothing lost, for I have nothing more to lose. *But I must save myself for all of you if at all possible. For that reason,* I prefer uncertain life to certain death.

Don't be angry with me, my sweet, beloved darling, that I write such ugly things to you; I don't believe that they frighten you. You know how things are; you certainly know even more than you want to admit to me, because you want to show consideration for my feelings. You don't need to do that—I have come to terms with everything, have

27. [Meant here is Heinrich Himmler, whose full title after 1936 was *Reichsführer-SS und Chef der deutschen Polizei*, or "Reich Leader of the SS and Chief of the German Police."]

seen and experienced so much here that there is only *one thing* left that would upset me, and that would be if something happened to you. *That* must not happen; I entreat my Lord God every day that it won't! *And for that reason, the thought, too, of you and your freedom and good health is more important than help for me.* Always remember that, please, please! Don't think that now, because I am past a certain point, I might have become indifferent. To the contrary, I *want* indeed to defend myself, but there is now no longer any other means than the *immediate* new illness. For they have everything, but everything, in their hands. Who the traitor is, I do not know; in the last analysis, it also doesn't matter to me at all.

I have heard through Sonderegger today that Eberhard[28] too was arrested, probably in September among our own abroad [!]. I don't understand that at all now any more. By the way, he is connected with me in no way at all. Sonderegger asked only how it happened that he has lived with us; apparently, he knows nothing of the fact that he is the Schleichers' son-in-law. Also, the acquaintance with P. is *not* valued highly by Sonderegger; Sonderegger spoke about P., whom I "certainly knew by name, at least." P., by the way, appears to have given evidence clumsily about Dietrich, who then, for his part, referred again to me as a source—a string of testimonies that are played against each other not unskillfully. I believe I can no longer help very much.

The arrangement is the following: Red means infected food (ink spot on container). I always check thermos and container; in other respects, too, I examine carefully; you do the same! If there is written on a wrapping "Greetings from . . . " (there doesn't need to be any exclamation mark or underlining with it), then a message is inside. If you [mark] the things otherwise (e.g., "food," "coffee," etc.), do it only so that I see who is at home. All other arrangements remain valid (if possible, inscriptions, lists of contents, etc., by the three of you, but in any case *your* writing, etc.).

My darling, I would like so very much to write you a love letter, and there are always these distasteful things. But we must manage them together, and since I am no longer alone, can write to you, hear from

28. Eberhard Bethge had been arrested in October 1944 as a soldier in Italy and had been brought to the prison at Lehrter Street 3.

you, I believe too that we'll make it! I believe there are very, very few men who are as happy and as rich as I am. The life, the many, many fates that have passed by me in the last half year have taught me that, *still* more than I already knew it. The happiness and the riches of my life, they are you, you, you! You see, I have considered whether I ought to play the harmless cheerful spirit, whether I should not let you share in the thoughts I have *now.* I believe it would be an injustice. You have a strong heart, and you will, I think, want rather to live *with* me than *next* to me. Or is all that only very egoistic? I, in any case, am wonderfully strengthened in the feeling that now you know me better. I am quite reasonable, do not want to take this path too often, want to keep to myself much of what I experienced and experience, to tell later on. But I *had* to get some things off my chest and this above all: as long as we still are able to act, *we must act.* The war, the SS can thwart our plans at any time, and *I fear being evacuated from Berlin.* I would like by all means to remain here in Berlin. As close as possible to all of you; and as long as that lasts, I am also not quite yet at the mercy of those guys. Everything ends again and again with the solution: new illness! The lot of our parents is terribly hard. I would like so much to help— can I do it another way?

My angel, my all! That you love me; have I deserved it? It is such a great happiness; I would like to sink to my knees before you and thank you for it. God will fulfill this wish for me!

Kisses!! Hans

Must still send you a love greeting. Once started, I should go all the way. *I destroyed your letter immediately,* after I knew it almost by heart. My sweet angel—whenever I hear about the many others, then really no one has it so good as I do; no one has such a wife as I, and if I sometimes was beastly and unfair and hurried and had "no time" to show you how much I love you, to show you *that* I love you, you have nevertheless always known that, haven't you? Perhaps Maas[29] was entirely right: with what you mean to me, and the children, and what I have achieved outwardly, I surely could be the happiest human being under God's sun. Why this self-occupation with general things?—but

---

29. See p. 65 n. 17 above.

they are just thoughts that also go away again. Oh, I would like to be able to think them through with you once, to be able once to express what I really think! Just this one thing more now: I agree that your solution of the inscription problem is *much* better than my suggestion. So, "food," "coffee," means: whoever has written it is at home and chipper. "Food," "coffee" (with exclamation mark following) means: news. So "Greetings from . . ." is entirely unnecessary. *Otherwise, we stay with the previous arrangements.* Please be careful, all of you. The Koch daughter [Brigitte][30] too has now been arrested because it is believed that she knows where Gisevius[31] is. The children realize, of course, that they *absolutely* must say nothing. *Renate too!* My darling, love me the way I love you—it must turn out well. Somehow. I believe that. . . . Kisses, my all!

                                                                              Hans

[Approved Letter]

                                              Berlin
                                              [Prinz Albrecht Street 8]
                                              15 March 1945

My dearly beloved darling,
    Chris undoubtedly was here yesterday and brought your wonderful package. A thousand thanks. There were again such dear domestic things in it, and the miracle of the matches. Don't be angry if I just ask for them in general. They are so very necessary here, above all at night for the candle, and when the lights to out, which is after all often the case when there is an alarm. If you would think about washcloths, that

----

30. Brigitte Koch was the daughter of lawyer Dr. Hans Koch, who defended Martin Niemöller at his trial, met with Dietrich Bonhoeffer, Hans von Dohnanyi, and Eberhard Bethge at Ettal in the winter of 1940–41, and was arrested in January 1945 because he had given shelter to Dr. Gisevius. He too was executed just before the end of the war.

31. Hans Bernd Gisevius, during the War active on behalf of the *Abwehr* in the consular service in Switzerland and a member of the resistance group around General Oster. On 20 July he found himself in Berlin, spent several months in hiding, and was able to escape to Switzerland in January 1945.

would also be very nice; mine are now already very much in need of repair—but all of this is, after all, not important. I would like so much to hear something from you once—since the letter of 27 February, which was read to me, there has been no more news. Did you receive the small sketches that were delivered to the children eight days ago yesterday? I would so much like to know what your opinion of them is. Little Klaus must come home now at least for a few days. Excuse my awkward writing; my eyes sometimes don't want to work right. My eyes still give me some difficulties. But after all, that doesn't matter. It is just necessary to wait a bit. It will be all right, and I can read too. Have I already asked how things are now with Chris's school? And with Barbie's interpreter's work. Can you write to me about that? I have so much that I would like to know. All my thoughts revolve around that. We live, after all, with each other, don't we? But my fantasies are just not exact enough for me to visualize everything the way it is. I am doing quite well—you needn't worry at all. Write to me about what everything looks like in the house, what you all are doing— it is such a hard time for you, for everyone. Papa's birthday is just around the corner; I think of the parents so much; how is Mama? Everything all right at Friedrichsbrunn? Hug the children. I press you to my heart!

Your husband

[Approved Letter]

[Prinz Albrecht Street 8]
15 March 1945

Dear Mr. Sonderegger:

Would you please forward the attached letter to my wife? Have you received any letters from my wife? I would be very thankful if I could receive them.

I had hoped to be able to give you the letter myself. I am so grateful to you that you take consideration of my condition. But we must even so make progress, since you are bound in regard to a time limit. Because of my stupid collapse from the day before yesterday, time has

now been lost again. But now, of course, everything is again somewhat OK and we really must make headway. In any case, we must find
a way to reach the goal that has been given you. And I would like to do
my part in this, as much as I possibly can. If I am sleeping, please wake
me up; I have already told you that recently.

   With sincere thanks,

                                          Your very obedient,
                                          von Dohnanyi

[Handwritten note from Dr. Tietze, the director of the Neurological
Department of the State Hospital]

   Conversation with Sonderegger on 6 April 1945, about eight o'clock
in the morning. Sonderegger stood in front of the hospital and waited
for a car that was supposed to come from Prinz Albrecht Street. I
wanted to see Dohnanyi. Sonderegger no longer lets me go to him and
involved me in a conversation that ran approximately as follows:

T: Do you want to start the trial now?
S: The affair is settled, you know.
T: Does that mean the end of Dohnanyi?
S: He is himself to blame. He has worked against the *Führer,* and yet
   had every chance. How could he work against the *Führer,* who has
   given him such a well-paid position (he means the position as Reich
   judicial counselor)? Dohnanyi's attitude was ungrateful!
T: Do you want to destroy him?
S: Evasive answer, then: We know that he was the brains of 20 July.
T: Where are you going with him?
S: I don't know that yet.
T: Do you already have the indictment then, and will a trial still be
   started?
S: We have, you know, everything against him in our hands; we need
   nothing more at all.
T: Does that mean death?
S: A shrug of the shoulders.

[Christine von Dohnanyi to her son Klaus in Bundorf/Franken]

[Berlin-Dahlem
July 1945]

My dear boy,

I hope this letter reaches you. For how long a time have I no longer been able to write to you and only heard of you through Grandma and Uncle Karl-Friedrich. If you are with Maria, you will by now surely have heard about the events in the family, and there remains nothing more to say about them than that we must bear bravely what all of them have taken upon themselves. About Father, I heard nothing factual. The last is that he was hauled away from a special bunker in Sachsenhausen, where he was brought on 6 April, and since 15–16 April there has been no further trace of him. So I have little hope that he is still alive. Papa himself firmly expected that the Gestapo would murder him. On 5 April, I saw him once again secretly with Tietze in the State Hospital. He was very calm, asked that his greetings be conveyed to all of you, and was in good humor, as always. When we see each other, I'll tell you everything. You too will not have had many more hopes, and will reckon with everything. Be brave, my good child; your father was too. I believe it is right of you to remain there in the south a little longer. Don't run any risks on the trip home. Should you have the chance to speak with Mr. von Sch[labrendorff][32] himself, who will deliver this letter to you, then ask him for advice. I am often uncertain whether under present circumstances it would not be good if we all attempted to go to the west, but one cannot make any plans as long as one does not know on what scale one will be able to live.

From Aunt Sabine and Uncle Gert came news.[33] In England there was also a wonderful church service for Klaus and Dietrich, about which they told us. Would you have the desire to go to school in England for a while? You cannot, after all, put an end to your learning yet, or do you really think of staying with agriculture, even now when you probably will not later be able to own your own land? And even

32. Lawyer Fabian von Schlabrendorff.
33. From Oxford.

then you ought to be able to study agriculture, and you don't as yet have your *Abitur.*

I will see to it that I can speak with your director, but up to now all of Potsdam has been blocked off because of the conference.[34]

Chris has a few private lessons and is not yet back in school, because we now live in Dahlem, Bachstelzenweg 5. Our house was confiscated by Russians and occupied for seven weeks. So I am practically bombed out; that is, all that is lacking is the tidiness of a fire. I am really unhappy most of all about the treatment of our books, which were "no good" and as a result were thrown into the cellar.

But everything else really doesn't affect me any more. One learns not to value transitory goods too highly.

Hans-Walter[35] came back from captivity under the Americans in good health. He is looking well and has not gone through too much, although he also did not have it very good.

I hope that you don't have any overly strenuous activity. You will, of course, get plenty to eat there, and that is quite a lot. Here the fat and sugar problems especially are a real calamity.

Now, farewell, my dear darling. May God help you in these terrible times to find the right path. All of you have good blood and a good heritage from your father in you, and you will be worthy of him. That is my comfort and my hope.

Farewell. Tell Maria that I think of her with all my heart. Perhaps you will talk to her sometime, after all, in the next few days. How much I would like to talk with her someday.

God preserve all of you. I embrace you.

Your Mama

34. The Potsdam conference, from 17 July to 2 August 1945.
35. Hans-Walter Schleicher.

JUSTUS
DELBRÜCK

Born 25 November 1902 in Berlin—1920, after the *Abitur*, employed in the Ruhr district as a miner—legal studies at Heidelberg and Berlin—1930, marriage to Ellen von Wahl—1933, government assessor in the office of the district president in Stade, then senior government counselor in Lüneburg—1936, departmental chief with the Reich Industrial Group—1939, fiduciary director of a cloth factory in the Niederlausitz—from 1940, active on the Canaris staff—arrested in early August 1944—during the final engagements of the war in Berlin at the end of April 1945, released from prison, yet shortly thereafter taken into custody by the Soviet side and finally transferred to the prison camp at Jamlitz, where he died at the end of October 1945.

Reminiscence

Between life and death in the prison at Moabit, Justus Delbrück wrote, "If God desires, he can say more through the death of a human being than through his life." Those were words of encouragement for the path he saw before him.

Justus Delbrück was born on 25 November 1902 in Berlin. His

father, the historian Hans Delbrück, had, as did the entire Delbrück family, deep feelings of solidarity with the Prussian-German Empire and was deeply disappointed by the collapse of 1918. Yet he acknowledged democracy to be the given form for Germany in that historical moment and showed the greatest respect for Ebert's point of view.

The young Justus Delbrück did not cling to what was lost. He also did not bemoan the dwindling away of the material foundations of the bourgeoisie in the period of inflation but rather saw in it an opportunity to free one's view and one's hands for the genuine concerns of life. Joy at everything that was genuine and honest was a basic feature of his nature.

Justus Delbrück shaped his life with his independent mind. When he was eighteen and had passed his *Abitur*, he went to the Ruhr district in order to work in the mines until the beginning of his university studies. And later, during the semester vacation, he once again did mining work, essentially out of social interest, in the Zwickau coal district.

Having occupied himself intensively with Mommsen, Ranke, and Hegel during his high school years, he wrote regarding his choice of his life's profession, "As much as history interested me, I did not want to devote my life to research. As highly as I valued the world in books, yet I wanted just as much not to have an effect through books but rather from person to person." To him, this wish was "a consequence of the Christian truth."

He studied law in Heidelberg and Berlin, and entered the career of a civil servant. About his relationship to the civil service profession, he said, "One reason I have not felt unfree even as a civil servant is that I have never made my happiness dependent upon a career. . . . So I was already convinced as a student that it makes no difference whether one leaves to posterity, as a minister like my Uncle Clemens Delbrück, a Reich insurance system or, as a lower court judge in a city or in the country, a series of good rulings and especially a good memory in the hearts of people. In this I see, also among civil servants, the real meaning of life."

When Hitler took over power in 1933, Justus Delbrück was a government assessor in the office of the district president in Stade; he went from there to Lüneburg as a senior government counselor, yet in 1936 gave up public service, which with the political development, had lost the "real meaning of life" for him. After three years' work as a departmental chief with the Reich Industrial Group, he took over a cloth factory in the Niederlausitz in a fiduciary capacity but then was drafted into the *Abwehr* in 1940 and worked there, closely associated with Dohnanyi, on the Canaris staff. He used every possible opportunity in Berlin to keep in contact with the friends with whom he felt himself politically and humanly bound. Among them, Klaus Bonhoeffer was his closest friend.

With heart and spirit, in responsibility and action, Delbrück was a member of the circle of resistance, and of those planning for the period "afterwards." He was, in the process, conscious of the far-reaching significance of the decisions that were made there. The compass guiding his judgment was alone his conscience, yet careful consideration and sober objectivity directed his conduct and action. Essential features of his character were a tendency toward total immersion and his search for truth, for the Spirit of God. Out of these grew love, understanding, and a deep desire for justice for all people. During his imprisonment, he made the decision to convert to Catholicism.

After the action of 20 July 1944, Justus Delbrück was arrested early in August. He succeeded, however, in dragging out his legal proceedings. After eight months of uncertainty and constant threat, he was released during the conquest of Berlin, since he had not yet been condemned.

With the words, "I've made it; I'm back again!" which he entered in his diary on 30 April 1945, he greeted his restored world. But the thought of his imprisoned friends, for whose return he hoped in vain, drove him about in a restless search.

Then after two weeks occurred his rearrest through a Soviet officer—allegedly for only three days, for the purpose of giving details about the resistance movement and the Canaris group. But Justus Delbrück did not return. At the end of October 1945, weakened through his imprisonment, he succumbed, according to the report of a fellow prisoner, to a sudden attack of diphtheria in the camp at Jamlitz near Lieberose in the Niederlausitz.

Annedore Leber

[From his prison diary]

[Lehrter Street 3]

20 August 1944–25 April 1945

In the Zurich novella by Keller,[1] I find the concluding words from the *Sachsenspiegel*, the oldest German law book, from the Middle Ages:

There is no one so unjust that it does not seem to him unfair when one does him an injustice. Therefore, one requires wise speech and considerable skills in order to apply them in the law. Whoever at all times speaks according to the law makes for himself many an enemy. To him the honest man should happily submit himself, for the sake of God's and his honor, and for the salvation of his soul. May the benevolent God grant to us that we, thus, love justice in this world and weaken injustice in this world, that we have our enjoyment of Him when body and soul depart from each other.

This for the boys, whether they become jurists or go through the world otherwise as men.

That is really the beautiful thing about the Psalms, that they express this human distress so completely: "I believe, therefore I speak. But I am sore afflicted" (Psalm 110).

It could, after all, be true that our Evangelical hymns seem so dry because they start from a false security. In that, one must agree with Keller. Our church trumpets forth faith in our ears like 2 + 2 = 4, just as though it were only a simple matter of grasping it with our understanding. But it's not that way at all. The psalmist wrestles with faith like Jacob with the angel—"I will not let you go unless you bless me" —and that's the way it is!

[On Dostoevski's *The Brothers Karamazov*]

What Alyosha, the youngest brother, says at the end about education is quite true and a consolation in these wild and educationless times:

1. [Gottfried Keller (1819–90) was born and died in Zurich although he spent a number of years in Germany. He is known for his use of the novella form. His two-volume *Zurich Novellas* (1878) is referred to here by Delbrück.]

Then know that there is nothing which would be higher, stronger, healthier, and more useful for life than a good remembrance from childhood, from the house of one's parents. A lot will be said to you about your education, but a beautiful and holy remembrance, which one still keeps for himself from the time of childhood, can often be the best education of all. If the human being has many such remembrances from youth, then he is saved for his entire life. And even if only one, single, good remembrance remains in his heart, then this, too, can serve sometime for his salvation.

[Letter to his son]

[Lehrter Street 3]
Advent 1944

Dear Klaus,

You will soon be fourteen years old already, and I think of the time when I became fourteen; that was on 25 November 1916, in the midst of the First World War. There were, of course, no bombs in Berlin at that time, and so we didn't need to leave our nice house in Grunewald. But otherwise, it was similar and, as far as food is concerned, more difficult; in any case, I have a not very pleasant memory of the "rutabaga winter." The tires on the bicycles were requisitioned, and that distressed me the most. Then I see us in the bitterly cold winter of 1917, crouching around gas and petroleum burners in two rooms. We boys then were also always busy in some way, with collections and in other ways, although it was not so thoroughly organized like today.

I started farm work for the first time in the fall of 1917, that is, when I was fifteen years old. We dug potatoes on a state demesne in the Neumark; I was the youngest and found it quite strenuous.

It was nicer then the next summer, even though the hours were long, the heat tremendous, and the shoes hard and bad.

But I stayed on a bit longer with two comrades and we wiped out thirty pounds of potatoes a day. On Sunday, we were invited to dinner at the estate, and there there was a real roast and I was angry with myself everytime that I didn't have a real appetite built up during the week, because on Sunday, breakfast too was good and late.

In the last days of the war, we were also mobilized as medics. We waited for the hospital trains at the train stations and helped as stretcher bearers with the transportation to the hospitals.

At school there were always new substitute teachers as replacements for those who were drafted. That was not very conducive to learning but contributed to our amusement. Thus, I still remember one slight man, the teacher Henri, who loved to recite poems, although he had a lisp and spat. Of course, we cheered him on in his enthusiasm and rewarded him with frenzied, roaring applause, so that I was really sorry for the little fellow. But after the lesson, he said to me and some of my comrades that he really had been happy with the day, that he absolutely had not expected such enthusiasm! I still have to laugh about that today. Luckily for me, my father did not attach special significance to good marks, but one had to make sure that a grade did not have to be repeated and when I once had difficulties with an unpleasant teacher, he told me the admonition from old Uncle Henning to his son Ottobald: "Consider your teachers to be wild animals, and try to cope with them!"

"I'm not the one telling you that," he added, upon the concerned objections of my mother, "I'm only telling you about it."

But besides that, there was otherwise a nice free tone between teachers and students in our school, so that special caution was not necessary in order to get along with the teachers. And in the upper grades there were even two excellent teachers, Martin Havenstein and Walter Kranz, from whom one could learn something. Only, I lacked too much in the fundamentals of Greek, just as in general I regret not having learned more at school; in the natural sciences too I would like to know more.

Thus, it surely lies in your own interest to learn everything at school one can learn, for much is hard to make up for later.

But now comes the time too when your own interest for this or that area will awake in you. Stick with it then; that is still more important than hard work at school. When I was fifteen to sixteen years old and began to be interested in history, I still remember that I made out for myself a schedule in Mommsen's Roman history, a number of pages that I wanted to read daily. Between the parts that interested me, there was also much I had to force myself to read. Among belles-lettres, it was the historical novels and the poems of Conrad Ferdinand Meyer that excited me. Since then, however, I've not taken them up again. Lene just sent me something by him, and among the poems there are the good old familiar ones, and again I find the ballad of the death of Vercingetorix very beautiful.

I also read the classics of Goethe, Schiller, and even Shakespeare with the feeling that I must have read them much too early. One ought not force oneself to read these things. The wonderful world of poetry comes to us when we have need of it.

But, when you find a poem beautiful, then learn it by heart. It is a boundless pleasure to sense the euphony in beautiful language, a pleasure I enjoy very much just now in learning one scene after another from Faust.

In November 1918, I was just about to experience my sixteenth birthday. Along with the Prussian-German Empire, the *Reich* with which the Delbrück family had had deep feelings of solidarity for generations broke apart, and my father's seventieth birthday on 11 November 1918 was like a wake. But when one is young, one cannot just mourn about what is lost, and I sensed something new. With the inflation that now commenced, the material foundations of the bourgeoisie were also lost to a great extent, and precisely therein did I find something that aroused my imagination. I still remember that I once said to my father that I had the vision of the time before 1918 as a gilded, white-enameled nursery, and now I found things better.

I had gladly taken upon myself the restrictions of the war out of patriotism—up to the point of attempting to run barefoot—and now old Socrates was a beloved model for me. His teaching that one never ought to attach great importance to the opinion of the crowd and that one always has to heed the judgment of the Good and Noble—or of the Beautiful, as the Greeks expressed it—I interpreted for myself in such a way that everyone who found fault with my old military jacket with open-wing collar, my untidy puttees, my long, uncut hair just did not belong to the Good and the Noble, which alone mattered.

At school, in the last years, I felt quite good. I used the opportunity to choose electives, which were introduced on an experimental basis at that time in individual subjects, to learn more Greek; and even if I was weak in grammar up to this point, yet my interest was acknowledged. To be sure, I attended the other blessings of the revolution—the students' council and the plenary assembly in the auditorium—only to make fun of them and to produce confusion.

In February 1920, I made my *Abitur* after some effort, and then, with disdain of all forms, I did not at all wait for the ceremonial farewell in the auditorium but rather in the dark morning hours I set myself in a fourth-class railroad car in order to travel to Dortmund. There I wanted to work in the mines until the beginning of the semester.

At that time the passenger trains still had the fourth class; the cars, like baggage cars, had no compartments but only a bench along each wall. My father would have given me a third-class ticket for the express train, with which I would have got there in half the time, but that was in no way possible. A decent human being could not travel in the third, or perhaps, second class; only hidebound Philistines traveled there. In the fourth class on the other hand rode the free people, who helped each other out and conversed in a friendly way. In Dortmund, I looked for accommodations for myself and went up and down flights of stairs. Then, finally, a worker ran after me on the street and said that the woman in the apartment above wanted to take me in after all; she had thought that otherwise I would go to the people on the lower floors of the house, and they were bad people, and I could sleep with him in his room.

So then I had quarters at Tremonia Street 30. I have forgotten the name of those good people; the man was a washroom superintendent at the Tremonia mine. Then I too got my miner's lamp and rode along into the pit. Twenty-four people always squatted down in the two levels of the mine cage, silent, with the lamp between their knees, and then with a whoosh it went six hundred meters down, so that your ears buzzed. Below, I had to walk still a few more minutes, often stooping over, until I came to the tenth tunnel, to a small coal elevator; here, first of all, we took a short break until the last person had come down— seven hundred workers descended in twenty minutes. And then I remained alone, for my task was to pull the empty cars in and the full ones out, and with a drawbar on the constantly running cable, to send them on their way.

At first I was assigned to the afternoon shift, when there was more construction and less coal was produced; so I had a comfortable life, and that annoyed me tremendously, for I had not come here, after all, just to earn the money for my studies but rather I also wanted to work at something hard, since I, of course, had never got to know the trench.

Afterwards then I also got into the morning shift, and there things went briskly, and one had to be careful there wasn't any breakdown because of a derailment while pulling the cars out, for the production and harmony among the workers depended on the flow of the empty cars.

Still, my greatest desire, to come before the coal myself along with the others, was not fulfilled here. I got to know that only later, in the old Wilhelm Pit at Zwickau. There, I lay with others in a hot coal seam, only one meter high, and worked with ardor and pick and shovel in time with the rhythmical clatter of the coal conveyor. And when a worker said to me, "You're really no slouch!" that was the most marvelous honor.

But while I was so proud to be a miner, I could not get over how the workers themselves spoke about how despised the station of the miners was, and that they carefully hid their trademark, the blue thermos bottle, when they walked through the city.

And still something else occurred to me. My fellow miners could not stand the sight of me without a hat, and finally one of them gave me an old black felt hat, which I then actually wore in the pit. Also, I was soon asked why I didn't shave, for the young workers were proud to shave as soon as possible. My landlord, the washroom superintendent, was too embarrassed to walk along the street with an unwrapped loaf of bread. So I soon noticed that customs of this nature were observed here just as strictly as among the bourgeoisie. The characteristic freedom and openness in the worker's nature, in contrast to the middle-class citizen, lie not in less-established customs—where they are less established, it is not good—but rather in the fact that the manual laborer does not take himself and his work as seriously as does the civil servant his service or the merchant his business. A human being who takes himself seriously is not free; he must always take care that everyone else, of course, recognizes his importance too. I saw this later among the farmers in the Stade district too. The poor farmers of the high, dry coastal lands were at ease, open in their nature, and hospitable, while it was much more difficult to acquire a human relationship to the fat lowland farmers.

And among the intelligent people, it is as Claudius writes to his son, "If someone wishes to teach you, then see if he fancies himself to be something. If he fancies himself something, then let him go." Among the nobility, the motto is, Noblesse oblige.

For the summer semester, then, I went to Heidelberg. According to my view, joining a students' corps was out of the question. I never once ate lunch at the students' cafeteria but rather in the public soup kitchen, and instead of fencing I learned to box. But luckily for me, old Socrates had not scorned the drinking of wine; indeed, according to the report by Plato in the *Symposium,* he manifested an astonishing ability to hold his liquor at a banquet. So I enjoyed not only the Palatine, but also the sweet Greek, wine with my friends in the old wine pub in Neckargmünd. In the process, one could also gloriously disdain the beer guzzling.

At Pentecost, however, we hiked through the Black Forest to Lake Constance, the heavenly Lake Constance, and then farther, on side trips to Vorarlberg in the Alps. The most beautiful, however, is the Black Forest, with its green valleys, the thick, dark forests with the crystal clear streams, so wonderful for cookouts. It would be something if the good Lord permitted us to do it once again together!

As far as my studying is concerned, I began it immediately with some seriousness, for I had the feeling that I ought to compensate somewhat in consideration of my school experiences. So I pursued not only my love, history, which was joined now by philosophy, but also began early on to become engrossed in the law.

The fact that I studied law and *not,* in accord with fashionable sentiment, political economy or national economy was thanks to my father. "I wouldn't give you two cents for all that national economy," he said, and that was enough for me, and I am happy that I didn't waste any time with it at the university. I made up quite well for that later through newspaper articles and some books.

Law, however, is a difficult material and requires proper study—like Latin at school: take with you in Demin what you can; one does not make up for it later and yet would very much like to have it.

To be sure, legal thinking is chided a great deal, but it is the many poor jurists who have brought it into disrepute—the way the hypocrites have done to piety. I received my first notion of law thanks to the old book by Ihering about the spirit of Roman law. I read it during the semester break when I came out of the pit at Zwickau. But I had a so-called coach teach me legal practice as early as the second semester, a lawyer who possessed teaching talent and practical experience. Professors most of the time do not possess both, and I did not hear very many courses of lectures; I was also confirmed in this by my father, who told me of an observation by Gneist, a famous teacher of law from his youth. He had three kinds of students. The one kind he saw sitting before him daily and enthusiastically taking notes; they were the future judges of the lower courts. The second kind he saw twice during the semester, namely, at the first and last certification of attendance at the lectures, and they were the superior court and chief ministerial counselors. And the third kind? He didn't become acquainted with them at all, and they were the future ministers.

In the other subjects, I heard many interesting lectures but found no teacher who would have influenced me especially. By far the most I have acquired from books. My father was no longer lecturing at the university by 1918, but from him I obtained two orientation points for history and philosophy: Ranke and Hegel. In the course of the years, I have read everything by Ranke, and much of it several times, and always have had the greatest pleasure in it. I have not advanced as far as Hegel's difficult *Metaphysics.* I tormented myself with Kant, Fichte, and among the moderns, Rückert, and finally discovered that the question that occupied me the most, that of the freedom of the will, finds its solution in Christianity—in the paradoxical form in which Luther expresses it in the treatise on the freedom of a Christian: "A Christian is a perfectly free lord of all, subject to none. A Christian is a perfectly dutiful servant of all, subject to all."[2]

My father also asked me several times whether I didn't have the desire to take up his career and to make history my main subject of study. The major periods of world history, he said, were, of course,

2. [Luther's "The Freedom of a Christian" (1520) appears in Martin Luther, *Three Treatises,* rev. ed. (Philadelphia: Fortress Press, 1970), 261–316. The quotation cited here appears on p. 277.]

definitively illuminated through Ranke—with his own addition of the insertion of the condition of war into the political picture. But in many fields there was still much to glean. But as much as history too interested me, I did not want to devote my life to research and, at that, only to the gleanings. As highly as I valued the world in books, yet I wanted just as much not to have an effect through books but rather from person to person. My father, however, had doubts whether a civil-service career would suit me, because I lacked the necessary tractability. But as much as I also inherited from my father the spirit of independence, and even of contradiction, just as much, after all, have I not felt unwell in administration (with the exception of the years as a junior lawyer, in which the aversion to grade-school compulsion awoke with increased force). Many times I wanted it to be different, but I also was able to assert my will in the face of my superiors.

One reason I have not felt unfree even as a civil servant is that I have never made my happiness dependent upon a career. Philosophy again has helped me to this attitude. So I was convinced as a student already that it makes no difference whether one leaves to posterity, as a minister like my Uncle Clemens D., a Reich insurance system or, as a lower court judge in a city or in the country, a series of good rulings and especially a good memory in the hearts of people. In this I see, also among civil servants, the real meaning of life.

I still remember one time during my university study when my father's economic situation appeared so threatened by the progressing inflation that it was questionable whether I would be able to continue studying—whether, with the indications of general ruin, it would be worth it all. Then my father spoke of its perhaps being better if one became a moorland homesteader with a cow and goat, and in my fantasy I seriously considered this idea.

I especially remember one topic of conversation from the period after the War: coeducation. Grandfather was absolutely not in favor of it, and he did not like to see female students at the university, especially when they ran around in sandals without socks. Once—that was, however, probably before the War—he had said in a speech that it had not pleased him at all that at a university celebration "females" had sat among the students at the tables where there was drinking going on. Then afterwards, a leading woman came up to him and complained about the expression "females." But Grandfather laughed and, with raised finger, said, "Ladies, ladies," like the sergeant in *Minna von Barnhelm*.[3] Yes, she said, "ladies"; that is something entirely different.

So Grandfather did not like learned women, and especially not woman authors (with few exceptions). But that is something which is more for Feli—so, Feli, don't become too learned for me! What? You don't want that at all either? You want to be like the miller's daughter who didn't want to spin? My, just think of that! Then, take care that the prince comes too! And my little Hans, what do you want to be like? Like Hans, the hedgehog? Like Hans, the happy fool?[4] You have a cheerful heart, indeed, so there will be no trouble there. Just take care, all three of you, that you don't overlook the little gray man, or the fox who helps you take the golden bird from the golden castle. And don't fly away like the seven ravens, so that my sweet little Gabriele must search for you in all the four corners of the world.

Klaus, yes, and when you one day search for a wife, then you yourself must already know who the right one is. I am uneasy about just one thing, for, you know, you have a mother—such a mother, we both know that—and in the end you will compare, but don't do that if you really know what's good for you. You would never find a wife: the dear Lord does not repeat himself.

But, Feli and little Gabriele,[5] I can give you very good advice here. Put the guy next to your brother; if he can bear it, then you can be satisfied.

But I have strayed, and I read over what I have written down about my cult of primitivism, about the disdain of everything external. I am telling you this not so that you imitate me. We should enjoy all the things of the world—and among them, the so-called externals too—as they come to us. We just should not make ourselves dependent upon

3. [The German poet Gotthold Ephraim Lessing (1729–81) wrote a number of tragedies and comedies. *Minna von Barnhelm* (1763) was one of the most successful of the latter and is still performed on the German stage today.]

4. [Justus Delbrück in this passage and the sentences following refers repeatedly to characters in German fairy tales. The hedgehog, in the story of "The Hare and the Hedgehog," is particularly artful and full of tricks. The figure of Hans the lucky fool ("Hans im Glück") represents the simple human being who, despite foolishly losing all his material wealth, remains blissfully happy.]

5. The daughters Felicitas and Gabriele.

them, and only in this sense is it not bad that one show oneself once that these things really are not what matter most. Of course, the question still remains to be answered how much the good things offer real pleasure to us, and whether or not we sometimes let ourselves be deceived.

When I read how happily my grandfather, Berthold Delbrück, lived in Bergen on the island of Rügen as a district judge with his entire family in the small house you have seen, and with a probably meager stipend, without radio, auto, railroad, and also without central heating and an inside toilet, then the question appears to me quite obvious whether the marvels of technology have not in truth forged golden chains for us: they have brought us the big city with its tumult and in general a working day that is much too long. Earlier there were no vacations, but not because one worked more but rather because each day ended with the proper amount of leisure time.

There are really only two sources of human happiness: nature and conviviality—and have we progressed here? Or are we not rather in the situation of Faust, about whom the devil says,

> To him has destiny a spirit given,
> Which boundlessly and always presses forth,
> And whose precipitate ambition
> Bounds over all the joys of earth.

> Him I drag through furious living,
> Through shallow negligibility.
> He shall struggle, stare, and to me cling,
> And to his insatiability.

> Shall food and drink before gluttonous lips suspend;
> His refreshment shall he implore in vain,
> And had he also not himself to the Devil given,
> Still would have to fall to ruin!

And at the end, when the old Faust states his proud confession of earthly happiness, restlessly pacing forward, anxiety derisively replies,

> Who I once for myself possess,
> For him is all the world useless!
> Eternal darkness here come down!
> Sun rises not nor comes back down!

In perfectly external senses
Live there within all darknesses!
And this he knows about all wealth:
Not to possess it for himself.
Good luck or bad is a fancy;
He starves to death 'midst the plenty!
Is of the future just aware,
And master of it is he ne'er!

There are still other evil companions in life that tease and torment us. Also jealousy—the passion that zealously seeks what creates suffering[6]—is such a sinister companion.

Thus, the old holy man bows to the ground before the young Dimitri Karamazov in awe of future suffering, because his look reveals to him a noble but wild and jealous soul.

Now, we are more peaceful and do not have the wild blood of the Karamazovs, but we make things a bit difficult for ourselves even so. But I want to tell you, too, what good things I have read about jealousy. Jealousy is a necessary accompaniment to human love; every love wants to possess the beloved completely and exclusively, and the stronger the love, the more zealously does it keep guard that no third party interferes.

But what about this when we stand before God; does not all our love belong to him, and to all his creatures?

Here, we are all in the situation of the unrighteous steward.[7] We handle God's love as if it were our own property. We bestow it at our own discretion, and whomever we love we give the biggest place in our heart and not only excuse him what he owes us but also excuse him and justify his guilt before God. Thus, the steward too excuses on his own initiative something of the debt owed by the debtors to his master. But note, the master praises the steward because he has made friends for himself with the unrighteous mammon and he will charge to his account the treasures of love he has accumulated among his friends.

---

6. [The wordplay in German here should not be overlooked: "Auch die Eifersucht—die Leidenschaft, die mit Eifer sucht, was Leiden schafft— . . . "]

7. [The biblical passage under discussion here is Luke 16:1–13.]

So, it is marvelous to know that our love here is always a break-through to divine love—that, when we are united in love, nothing, nothing, nothing can separate us.

So, that's the way it is; that's the way I have written it. And now I hope very much that you can have it by your birthday, and that the good, best Aunt Lene picks it up and sends it to you. You know, it is good to have a sister. We go through our whole life with our sister. Husband and wife know their youth; the parents do not know our age. Sophocles has his Antigone say something like that. You must read that, too—the Greeks in general. But we can talk much more about that later.

Greet and kiss Muschka, my dear Feli, my little Hans, and the sweet, lovely Gabriele.

Your devoted father

[Letter to his wife]

[Marienburger Allee 43]
Monday, 30 April

Now my Ellen, my dearest, I've made it; I'm back again—the haz-ards of the war too are probably past. I am sitting in the Bonhoeffers' air-raid shelter—a Russian colonel has just come in. Only very seldom is German artillery still to be felt. So much has happened in these weeks, yet we don't know whether Klaus and Rüdiger, whether Diet-rich Bonhoeffer and Hans are still living; with Guttenberg[8] it is still likewise quite uncertain.

The last three days in prison brought the most terrible disappoint-ments yet. On Sunday, we expected the release of all of us together. Prof. Haushofer a week before had already had a list of names sent out secretly in order to secure identity papers for us immediately from the occupation authorities. Then plans were made concerning where we wanted to live and where we wanted to meet. Guttenberg and I wanted to go to Klaus's and live there. In the course of Sunday came the first releases, prisoners who were relatives. . . .

---

8. Karl Ludwig Freiherr von Guttenberg, editor of the *White Pages*.

DIETRICH
BONHOEFFER

Born 4 February 1906 in Breslau—from 1923 to 1927, theological studies at Tübingen and Berlin—1927, doctorate with "Sanctorum Communio"; 1930, postdoctoral dissertation: "Akt und Sein"—1930–31, study in the United States—1931, instructor on the Berlin theological faculty; at the same time, students' pastor and ecumenical youth secretary—1933, assumption of a pastorate in London—1935, beginning of the theological seminary at Zingst, then at Finkenwalde—1937, after closing of the seminary by the police, collective vicariates at Köslin and Gross-Schönwitz—1938, beginning of the contacts with the Canaris staff—1939, journey to the United States—1940, prohibition on speaking, and required registration with the police; reserve status in the *Abwehr* for occasional missions; several foreign journeys—early in January 1943, engagement to Maria von Wedemeyer; arrested 5 April 1943—executed 9 April 1945 at Flossenbürg.

Reminiscence

[To Ricarda Huch]

I want to try to tell, in order, what has remained in my memory about Dietrich's childhood especially. . . . After the nice games in the sandbox, the building of sand castles, volcanoes, marble courses,

95

magic fountains, and the care of the hobby horse began to lose their appeal, there came for Dietrich, together with me, his first school lessons. My mother unfortunately instructed us herself only very shortly since, with the five older brothers and sisters, she found no more time for it. Being sent to the "big school" pleased Dietrich only very little. He went unwillingly and also probably was teased somewhat because of his very light blond hair, which at that time was still long and had a pageboy cut. He said at that time, too, that a classmate had said of him that he "already had white hair"!

When the War broke out, Dietrich was eight years old. A little Japanese boy at that time attached himself to Dietrich and made Dietrich a present of beautiful wood carvings, of which Dietrich was very proud and which made him really happy, while on the other hand, he passed on to me unread the beetle and insect books the little Japanese boy gave him. For my grasshoppers, too, he had no interest. At that time he already played very nice piano for his age: "The Mill," the Schumann children's album, and "To Elise," for my mother. The school choir gave him pleasure, and in a school performance of Romberg's "Bell," he sang with a pretty voice the passage, ". . . then with the festive sound of joy it greets the beloved child!" During the last years of the War, we, that is, Dietrich, my younger sister, two neighbor boys, and I, played many wild games in the garden, also a lot of soldier. Dietrich was the captain and drilled with us and demonstrated for us all sorts of jumps and climbing about, really all of it tests of courage. He was always very fair while playing. With great enthusiasm, he built a subterranean cavern for us in which we sat and happily ate our snacks but also where we buried the little glories for which we scrimped and saved, like bonbons and chocolate, in order to be able to serve them to our brothers and sisters and parents at a cave party. In ball and running games, Dietrich was very good and unflagging. When sides were chosen, he actually always chose me, as his twin sister, first, although he could have chosen better players. At the same time, as late as his fourteenth year, he very much liked to win at his games.

Dietrich naturally liked very much to be at our country cottage at Friedrichsbrunn during the vacations. As a boy, he was a passionate picker of berries and, above all, mushrooms. He knew them all. He picked enormous numbers of lactarius and dried them for our father, who so much liked to eat mushroom soup. He was untiring in picking berries on the steep, sunny slopes between the shadeless hunting preserves, although the horseflies bit and the sun burned down on his head. For my sister and me, he tramped down all the stinging nettles, searched out good places for us, and—if he had found more than we—poured off some of his into our buckets. He pulled me up many a steep hillside and, to our relief, relieved us of a backpack or a coat with a friendly "Come, give it to me!" The matter-of-factness with which Dietrich held a book or a newspaper for one to read along with him so that one could read very easily, while he could read it only with great effort, was very characteristic of him.

It was in Friedrichsbrunn too where he began, at the age of thirteen, to devour the classics. Then in the evenings we many times read parts. He loved the book *Helden des Alltags*,[1] which was there and told about the courageous, selfless deeds of children who died doing them. On our trips in the Harz, Dietrich liked very much to make stops at Halberstadt and Quedlinburg in order to be in the cathedral for a few hours. The architecture of old cities and churches interested him quite early. He also loved the cities of Brandenburg, with their churches, very much.

When he came back from the Harz, he always looked forward very much to playing the piano. He filled up his free time with it and also, as a fourteen-year-old, thought about studying music. For a long time, Saturday evening was the "musical evening," when each of us children performed something. Dietrich very early played from memory and also quickly learned to accompany our mother quite well in her singing of Schubert, Beethoven, and Wolf *lieder*. He also once tried his hand at composition. The psalm lines "Why are you cast down, O my soul? And why are you disquieted within me? Hope in God, for we shall yet thank him for the help of his countenance"[2] he set to music for several voices but then let it lie, as well as a trio on the

1. [*Everyday Heroes.*]
2. [Psalm 42:5. The translation here follows the KJV and Sabine Leibholz's quotation of the passage.]

theme of the last of the *Müller Lieder*, "Gute Ruh, tu die Augen zu,"[3] which he rehearsed several times with my brother Klaus and me but then never took up again.

When Dietrich was fourteen, we both began our confirmation lessons. When and how his intention to study theology developed I cannot say exactly. In the confirmation lessons, he also got to know Hans von Haeften, and each of them got on well with the other. (He was the brother of Werner von Haeften, whom Hitler had shot along with Stauffenberg after 20 July.) Otherwise, Dietrich had no close friends. But he also didn't need anyone, because he lived so intensely within the circle of his brothers and sisters. At school, however, he was quite popular with the boys. Only during his university studies, to be sure, did he find a real friend.

But I should, after all, tell about his childhood. I want to say further that Dietrich always practiced my violin sonatas with me with great patience and kindness and never lost his self-control even with my repeated wrong entrances. Yet, he often had a sad, despairing look when a song was sung and someone started talking before he was able to complete his postlude.

After our brother Walter died in France at the age of eighteen, Dietrich read quite a bit. At that time we often went into one of the bookstores close by, where we browsed around and usually also found something we bought for our bookshelves with our allowance. Dietrich also was pleased by handsome editions. With reproductions, he was very critical. Sometimes he bought himself a nice reproduction in the Kaiser Friedrich Museum before he left it, as though he could not so suddenly tear himself completely away from all the beauty and had to take something of it home with him. Dietrich finished school effortlessly, almost casually.

After the *Abitur*, he invited me on a walking tour made possible by his graduation money, through the Thuringen Forest, which he didn't yet know.

In Meiningen, where we began our tour with heavy backpacks,

---

3. [Wilhelm Müller (1794–1827) was a poet who often put his poems together in song cycles. The collection of *Müller-Lieder* (1816) was set to music by Franz Schubert too. The title of the song here cited can be translated "Sweet Repose, Close My Eyes."]

there was early spring weather, but the Rennsteig still lay under snow and on the Inselsberg we got into deep snow and an icy storm, for which we were not equipped. I will never forget how touchingly Dietrich cared for me, wrapped up my things, and tramping on ahead, wanted to secure my every step in the snow, since we didn't have any snowshoes. Again and again he knocked off the crusts of ice from the hem of my dress and tried to protect me against the awful storm, although I didn't complain at all. We talked with each other a lot about the family and friends, about music, about the future, and were very happy together. We sang a lot while walking.

I must also say further that Dietrich enjoyed playacting. As a young boy, he adapted Hauff's fairy tales for us for performing, and later we played *Le malade imaginaire,* in which he played the part of Argan. A situation comedy always was great fun for him, and he had much understanding of theatrical staging and, quite early, a great deal of taste. With enthusiasm and pleasure, we performed *Die Journalisten,* by Gustav Freytag. With friends from school, he performed the *Weissen Fächer,* by Hofmannsthal, and many were impressed with the beauty and maturity with which he spoke the prologue and epilogue. Dietrich was very impressed at that time by his *Der Tor und der Tod,*[4] too. During his school days he liked very much to go to the theater, but not very much later on. Several times he exchanged a nice seat at the State Opera for two balcony seats and then invited me. We heard *Carmen* from standing room and enjoyed it very much.

Sabine Leibholz

(Encounters in Tegel)

At the gate I get a number and a pass. Broad paths between red walls; windows with bars behind yards enclosed by fences. I walk my bicycle—perhaps it is forbidden to ride it here. The air in the waiting room is even mustier than in the passageways, but of course I have

---

4. [Dietrich Bonhoeffer's theatrical experiences included performances of the fairy tales of Wilhelm Hauff (1802–27); of *The Journalists,* a comedy from 1854 by Gustav Freytag (1816–95); and of two works by the Austrian dramatist and Strauss librettist Hugo von Hofmannsthal (1874–1929): *White Fan* and *The Fool and Death.*]

known it now for weeks: "Without visiting permit, go directly through to package reception area." The waiting people cling to the narrow wooden bench close to the wall and hold their little cases and packages carefully, almost tenderly, on their laps. No one in the room is without a masked expression; no unnecessary word is spoken. . . .

It is my turn to hand over at the counter the things I am bringing for Dietrich. Thorough inspection. The periods beneath the letters—our code—with which the books that pass back and forth are marked, are never noticed. Renewed waiting until the call. Then there lie the things Dietrich just had in his hands: books, dirty laundry, empty waterproof paper containers that he carefully has preserved—valuable objects at that time, for it is forbidden to use glass and tin cans for the transport of food. Again a thorough inspection. A note in Dietrich's handwriting, to me a bit foreign because of its clear readability—certainly for the sake of the inspection. Requests for handkerchiefs, certain books, soap, or other permitted little things. No greeting; no signature. I am permitted to take note, to write things down. He must wait eight days for the desired articles.

I am just packing everything in the shabby case when one of those in uniform—later, I learn that he is Corporal Holzendorf—motions to me and says, "You still wanted to make a telephone call, didn't you?" Of course, why shouldn't I want to make a telephone call? Perhaps he has some message to deliver to me. Following behind him, through narrow gray-white passages. Wordless. Then he opens a door. "A quarter of an hour," he says, steps back, lets me enter, and closes the door behind me. In front of me stands my brother.

It is good that we have learned in our parents' house to remain outwardly in control of even our most intense feelings. But we remain mute in the first moment nevertheless, while we shake hands. Then I automatically lay my jacket over the telephone on the desk and explain my presence: "I am making a telephone call here, you know!" "I didn't know at all why I was called," says Dietrich, "That is, after all, awfully nice of Holzendorf." And with this adjective, used so readily by him earlier, our entire childhood and youth are again between us in the room, and the evil horror of these closed-up walls is as though swept away. If the corporal on duty in the detention prison at Tegel can be "awfully nice," then I have Dietrich before me unbroken; then he has kept his old obliging way of accepting and acknowledging human beings.

Now the questions about the condition of the family, especially about that of our imprisoned brother-in-law Hans von Dohnanyi, and my answers string themselves together in the high-speed manner of talking that is a matter of course for us brothers and sisters but that easily makes listening guests, even friends of the family, dizzy. It is good for the few minutes we have—how long can a telephone conversation in the prison last without being noticed, anyway?—that we have learned in our parents' house to say briefly and concisely only what is essential, though this short form of speech, like our reserve in expressing feelings, may appear harsh.

Most important are a few bits of news for our brother-in-law that emerged from the interrogations and that can be passed further on along hidden paths. Dietrich would like to know what we think of the situation. If we didn't know that even among ourselves wishes give rise to our thoughts, we would know better what we would have to think about the situation. So we agree that I speak from the point of view of the civilian opposition and the work in the church, he from that of the military detention prison: it cannot last much longer; every joint is creaking, economically, militarily, personally. "It cannot last much longer; hold out just a little bit more," smiles Dietrich, and then he asks about his godson, my Michael, and says that it had made such a strong impression on him from his last visit with us that the six-year-old sang from memory all the verses from the song "Warum sollt ich mich denn grämen" [Why then should I worry?] in his little bed in the evening. The little one, taking notice of our failure, recited the second verse to us especially loudly, since neither of us any longer had it ready and securely in memory: "Naked I lay on the ground; there I came; there I took my first breath; naked will I wander again, when I will fly from the earth like a shadow." "I, too, have now learned all the verses by heart," says Dietrich. I remember well the evening, the infant's voice in the dark. It touched us, but we had, thank God, no presentiment of how exactly it did so. Both of us now have all we can do not to break down, for the time is about to run out. Short messages, a few requests, "Tell us really what you need and would like to have; we certainly will not go hungry because of them; many friends want to help." Slowly the door opens, I slip into my jacket, Dietrich keeps his distance in case Holzendorf does not come alone. But he comes alone. "May God preserve you all in these air attacks!" "All of you here, too." Later, the really good, brave, and—one can certainly say here—noble Holzendorf, who attempted to make prison life easier for others too, becomes the victim of a bomb in an air raid. But only later. It happens two times more when I come to Tegel on Friday with my little case that I am permitted to "telephone," and find Dietrich in Holzendorf's room. Of course, he must maintain longer intervals in order not to attract attention.

But there is still another outlet for Holzendorf's resourcefulness in making us happy. While I pack up the things returned to me, I hear him call out, "Bonhoeffer, come down for exercise!" There is the big prison yard, and if I move really slowly, I come by it precisely when he comes out with his guard. So at least we see each other, nod very carefully, attempt to assure each other of our laboriously maintained confidence, through a glance, a movement, thoughts. . . .

Friday, 28 July 1944.[5] The way is very, very long this time on the bicycle from Dahlem to our parents' house at the Heerstrasse train station in order to pick up the latest news and the things for Dietrich, and then to Tegel. What may have changed for him, the nephew of the imprisoned City Commandant von Hase? Will the permission for reception of laundry, food, and smoking materials still remain for him? Will I be able to bring our parents some kind of news about him? Our friend Holzendorf has been dead since January. Nevertheless, Dietrich has been able now and then on Friday after getting his things, to take a half-hour walk in the courtyard—for a long time now no longer in the company of the lieutenant but rather with just a guard who, however, is well informed and a friend.

Admittance, delivery, inspection, waiting—inspection, return delivery. Everything runs like always. Now pack everything very slowly, in case he still comes down to exercise. Painstakingly, I unchain my bicycle and in the process look tensely to the prison yard.

5. After the failed attempt at an overthrow on 20 July.

Nothing. Laboriously, I fasten the case, push my bicycle away, a longing glance through the fence to the corner of the yard from which he is accustomed to come. Then I see him coming toward me very calmly along the broad path with his guard. It is good that in my parents' house, with seven big brothers and sisters, I learned actively to con my way through when what was important was to attain something. I must speak to Dietrich inconspicuously. Both valves are quickly removed from the bicycle, I lean it against the wall, make an effort with the pump, my back turned to the two who are coming closer. Now they are standing still behind me. It's working! "Had a breakdown? Can I help you?" asks the guard loudly, and Dietrich says softly, "We can talk, Mr. Knobloch is absolutely reliable." I express my thanks loudly and heartily, hand over pump and valves, interestedly bend over the bicycle, before which our good genius squats and enthusiastically does everything that is unnecessary. Dietrich stands, uninvolved, close by and talks without moving his lips. My answers are directed harmlessly, in a subdued tone, toward the bicycle as though they might have to do with suggestions for repair of the puncture. "No, our brother Klaus is free, but [Dietrich's fellow confirmand and friend] Hans von Haeften has been arrested along with his wife. He was still with us on Sunday for Holy Communion at the church in Dahlem. After it, he spoke quite calmly with us about his probable end. His brother was an adjutant with Stauffenberg. In the evening then we waited in vain for his promised visit." Dietrich is very concerned; his friend leaves five small children behind. Our brother-in-law Hans still lies in prison with paralysis after a severe case of diphtheria. That is now reassuring. Dietrich is informed about the fate of our uncle,[6] about everything the radio is able to report. He hears it in the guard room. The English station too. He is disturbed that so little notice is taken there of the entire event of the insurrection. For him no sharpening of conditions has made itself felt as yet. But he looks worse than he ever did before. "Everything will, of course, probably be different in the future." And then the wishes again: but perhaps now everybody will grasp what's going on; perhaps now it will end quickly, after all; the unrest is growing, you

6. General Paul von Hase.

know; too many have been touched. "There has never been so much rapping on the walls going on at night here as in the last few days," he says. Mr. Knobloch has used almost an hour to reinsert the two valves and to pump up the tires. I express my thanks heartily and innocently to the two gentlemen with a handshake, and walk my bicycle, without turning back, to the exit gate; the tears then roll down my face nevertheless. But that attracts no particular attention from the jailers here.

I am hardly conscious of the way home, so happy am I to be able to tell our parents that I have seen and spoken to Dietrich. "Rapping on the walls at night," I think; "among us it started with rapping on the walls." One day when we "three little ones" no longer slept in the same room, he declared to me and my sister Sabine, "During the day we think much too little about the dear Lord, and evenings after praying, I too think immediately about something else again and hear how you in the next room begin to chatter. Shall I, when in the evening the dear Lord comes to my mind, rap to you three times on the wall so that you too think about him?" Three raps on the wall— sometimes I can still hear them. I wonder whether they have oc- curred again to Dietrich too in his cell. On 28 July 1944, I met my brother Dietrich for the last time.

Susanne Dress

[Tegel]
21 July [1944][7]

Dear Eberhard, today I want to send you just a short greeting. I think you are here with us in your thoughts so often and so much that you will be glad for every sign of life, even when the theological discussion takes a rest for once. To be sure, theological ideas occupy me inces- santly, but then there also come hours in which one is satisfied with the unreflected-upon processes of life and faith. Then, one quite simply

7. On the day after the failed *Putsch*.

takes delight in the day's readings,[8] as I do especially in yesterday's and today's, and returns to Paul Gerhardt's beautiful hymns and is glad to have them.

In the last years I have learned to know and to understand more and more the deep this-worldliness of Christianity; the Christian is not a *homo religiosus* but rather plainly and simply a human being, as Jesus— in contrast, of course, to John the Baptist—was a human being. I don't mean the trivial and banal this-worldliness of the enlightened, the busy, the comfortable, or the lascivious, but rather the deep this-worldliness that is filled with discipline and in which the knowledge of death and resurrection is always present. I believe that Luther lived in this this-worldliness.

I remember a conversation I had with a young French pastor[9] thirteen years ago in America. We quite simply had asked ourselves the question what we really wanted to do with our lives. Then he said, I would like to become a saint (and I consider it possible that he has become one); that impressed me very much at that time. In spite of that, I disagreed with him and said something like, I would like to learn to have faith. For a long time I did not understand the depth of this contrast. I thought that I could learn to have faith in attempting to lead something like a holy life myself. As the end of this path, I wrote, I suppose, *The Cost of Discipleship*. Today I see clearly the danger of this book, although I stand behind it as before.

Later I learned, and I am learning it to the present hour, that one learns to have faith only in the complete this-worldliness of life. When one completely renounces making something out of oneself, whether one is a saint or a converted sinner or a churchman (a so-called priestly type!), a righteous person or an unrighteous person, a sick person or a healthy one—and this I call this-worldliness, that is, to live in the profusion of duties, problems, successes and failures, experiences and per-

---

8. 20 July: "Some trust in chariots, and some in horses; but we will remember the name of the Lord our God" (Psalm 20:8 [Psalm 20:7 (KJV)—TRANS.]). "If God be for us, who can be against us?" (Rom. 8:31). 21 July: "The Lord is my shepherd; I shall not want" (Psalm 23:1). "I am the good shepherd, and know my sheep, and am known of mine" (John 10:14).

9. Jean Lasserre.

plexities—then one throws oneself completely into God's arms; then one does not take one's own suffering seriously but, rather, God's suffering in the world; then one watches along with Christ in Gethsemane; and I think that that is faith, that is *metanoia*. And so does one become a human being, a Christian (cf. Jeremiah 45!). How could one become cocky about successes or lose faith when there are failures, if one suffers with God in the this-worldly life? You understand what I mean even if I say it in such a brief way. I am thankful that I have been permitted to learn this, and I know that I have been able to learn it only on the path along which I now have gone. For that reason, I think thankfully and in peace of what is past and present.

Perhaps you are surprised about such a personal letter. But if I want to say something like this for once, to whom else ought I say it? Perhaps the time will come someday when I can speak to Maria too in this way; I hope so very much. But I cannot burden her with this yet.

May God lead us cheerfully through these times, but above all, may he lead us to himself.

I was especially happy about your greeting, and I am glad that it is not too hot for all of you. Many more greetings should come to you from me. Didn't we actually travel this path more or less in 1936?[10]

Farewell, stay in good health, and don't let your hopes sink that we all will see each other again soon. I always think of you in faithfulness and gratitude.

Your Dietrich

STATIONS ON THE ROAD TO FREEDOM[11]

Discipline

If you set out to seek freedom, then learn above all things
to govern your soul and your senses, for fear that your passions
and longing may lead you away from the path you should follow.
Chaste be your mind and your body, and both in subjection,
obediently, steadfastly seeking the aim set before them;
only through discipline may a man learn to be free.

10. The journey to Italy is meant; see *Dietrich Bonhoeffer*, 627–28.
11. Written in Tegel after the failed *Putsch*.

Action

Daring to do what is right, not what fancy may tell you,
valiantly grasping occasions, not cravenly doubting—
freedom comes only through deeds, not through thoughts taking wing.
Faint not nor fear, but go out to the storm and the action,
trusting in God whose commandment you faithfully follow;
freedom, exultant, will welcome your spirit with joy.

Suffering

A change has come indeed. Your hands, so strong and active,
are bound; in helplessness now you see your action
is ended; you sigh in relief, your cause committing
to stronger hands; so now you may rest contented.
Only for one blissful moment could you draw near to touch freedom;
then, that it might be perfected in glory, you gave it to God.

Death

Come now, thou greatest of feasts on the journey to freedom eternal;
death, cast aside all the burdensome chains, and demolish
the walls of our temporal body, the walls of our souls that are blinded,
so that at last we may see that which here remains hidden.
Freedom, how long we have sought thee in discipline, action, and
    suffering;
dying, we now may behold thee revealed in the Lord.

[Accompanying lines to "Stations on the Way to Freedom"]

Dear Eberhard, I wrote these lines this evening in a few hours. They are quite crude, yet perhaps they will give you some pleasure, and they are, after all, something like a personal birthday present! Warmest greetings,

Your Dietrich

I see, early this morning, that I must alter these verses once again. Nevertheless, may they go out to you in raw form just the way they are. I'm no poet, you know!

[Tegel early October 1945]

JONAH[12]

In fear of death they cried aloud and, clinging fast
to wet ropes straining on the battered deck,
they gazed in stricken terror at the sea
that now, unchained in sudden fury, lashed the ship.

"O gods eternal, excellent, provoked to anger,
help us, or give a sign, that we may know
who has offended you by secret sin,
by breach of oath, or heedless blasphemy, or murder,

who brings us to disaster by misdeed still hidden,
so make a paltry profit for his pride."
Thus they besought. And Jonah said, "Behold,
I sinned before the Lord of hosts. My life is forfeit.

Cast me away! My guilt must bear the wrath of God;
the righteous shall not perish with the sinner!"
They trembled. But with hands that knew no weakness
they cast the offender from their midst. The sea stood still.

POWERS OF GOOD[13]

With every power for good to stay and guide me,
comforted and inspired beyond all fear,
I'll live these days with you in thought beside me,
and pass, with you, into the coming year.

---

12. On 29 September a discovery in the files by the Gestapo aggravated the situation
for the family. Early in October, D. Bonhoeffer gave up a plan of escape; about 5
October, then, this poem originated. On 8 October he was brought to the Gestapo's
basement prison on Prinz Albrecht Street and subjected to a new series of interrogations by the Reich Central Security Office. In the same month, Klaus Bonhoeffer,
Rüdiger Schleicher, and E. Bethge came to the Reich Central Security Office prison at
Lehrter Street 3.

13. From Prinz Albrecht Street at the end of December 1944, on the occasion of his
mother's birthday on 30 December, and for his fiancée.

The old year still torments our hearts, unhastening;
the long days of our sorrow still endure;
Father, grant to the souls thou hast been chastening
that thou hast promised, the healing and the cure.

Should it be ours to drain the cup of grieving
even to the dregs of pain, at thy command,
we will not falter, thankfully receiving
all that is given by thy loving hand.

But should it be thy will once more to release us
to life's enjoyment and its good sunshine,
that which we've learned from sorrow shall increase us,
and all our life be dedicate as thine.

Today, let candles shed their radiant greeting;
lo, on our darkness are they not thy light
leading us, haply, to our longed-for meeting?—
Thou canst illumine even our darkest night.

When now the silence deepens for our hearkening,
grant we may hear thy children's voices raise
from all the unseen world around us darkening
their universal paean, in thy praise.

While all the powers of good aid and attend us,
boldly we'll face the future, come what may.
At even and at morn God will befriend us,
and oh, most surely on each newborn day!

[Prinz Albrecht Street]
28 December 1944

Dear Mama, to my great joy, I have just received permission to write to you for your birthday. I must do it in a bit of a hurry since the letter is supposed to go out immediately. Really I have only one single wish, and that is to be able to make you happy in some way in these days that are so gloomy for you both. Dear Mama, you must know that every day I think of you and Papa a countless number of times and that I thank God that both of you are there for me and for the whole family.

I know that you always have lived only for us and that you have not had a life of your own. It is for this reason that I can experience everything I experience only together with both of you. It is very great comfort for me that Maria is with you. I thank you for all the love that in the past year has come to me in my cell from you and that has made each day a little easier for me. I believe that these difficult years have bound us still closer to each other than ever before. I wish for you and Papa and Maria and us all that the new year brings us a ray of hope at least now and then and that we will be able to rejoice together once again after all. May God keep you in good health!

I greet you, dear Mama, and think about you with my whole heart on your birthday.

Your grateful Dietrich

[Prinz Albrecht Street]
17 January 1945

Dear Parents, I am writing to you today because of the *Volksopfer,*[14] and would like to ask you to make my things available in their entirety. It's been reported that even a tuxedo would be accepted; please give mine. I also have a leftover felt hat and a salt-and-pepper suit that is too small, as well as a pair of brown oxfords. Dear Mama, you have a better idea than I do now of what I have. *In short, give without reservation whatever is needed in any way!* If you are in doubt about something, perhaps you could telephone Commissar Sonderegger! I have, of course, learned in the past two years how little a human being can make do with. Here in the inactivity of a long imprisonment, one especially has the need to do what is possible within narrow limits for the whole. All of you will feel the same way. If one thinks of how many people daily now lose everything, then one really does not have any claim at all anymore on any possession at all. I know that you think the same way, and I myself too would like ever so much to take part in the matter! Will Hans-Walter really fly now to the east? And Renate's

14. In the sometimes open-ended series of interrogations in the Reich Central Security Office, this "national offering" or *Volksopfer,* for which Goebbels made propaganda, provided an opportunity for this last letter. See *Dietrich Bonhoeffer,* 1012.

husband? Thank you very much for your letter; I thank Maria, too, *very* much for her Christmas letter! Letters here are read until they are known by heart!

Just a few requests: There were unfortunately no books delivered for me today. Commissar Sonderegger would accept them even between visiting hours if Maria brings them! I would be very grateful for them. Also matches, washcloth, and towel were lacking this time. Excuse me for saying this; everything was otherwise so splendid! Thank you very much! Could I please . . . have toothpaste and a few coffee beans? Dear Father, could you send from the library H. Pestalozzi, *Liehnhard* and *Abendstunden eines Einsiedlers;* P. Natorp, *Sozialpädagogik;* Plutarch, *Grosse Männer: Biographien?*[15] I am well. Just stay healthy! Thank you very much for everything. To Maria, many greetings and thanks! Also to all the brothers and sisters and to the mother-in-law. I greet you all from the bottom of my heart.

Your grateful Dietrich

Please deliver letter paper too to Commissar Sonderegger.

15. [The books Dietrich Bonhoeffer requested from his father were *Liehnhard and Gertrud* (1781–87) and *The Evening Hours of a Hermit* (1780) by the Swiss writer and social reformer Johann Heinrich Pestalozzi (1746–1827); *Social Education,* by the educator and philosopher Paul Natorp (1854–1924), who also commented on Pestalozzi's work; Plutarch's *Lives.*]

THEREAFTER

[Karl-Friedrich Bonhoeffer, for his children]

[Leipzig]
June 1945[1]

. . . I want to tell you about all of that. Why? Because my thoughts now are there, there in the ruins where no news penetrates through to us, where just a quarter-year ago I visited Uncle Klaus, condemned to death, in the prison. The Berlin prisons! What did I know of them just a few years ago, and with what other eyes have I looked at them since. The Charlottenburg Detention Prison, in which Aunt Christel was imprisoned for a time; the Tegel Military Detention Prison, in which Uncle Dietrich sat for a year and a half; the Moabit Military Prison with Uncle Hans; the SS prison of Prinz Albrecht Street, where Uncle Dietrich was held half a year behind bars in the cellar; and the prison of Lehrter Street, where Uncle Klaus was tortured and Uncle Rüdiger was tor-

---

1. The family had been evacuated to Friedrichsbrunn. The transfer of Leipzig out of American into Soviet hands was imminent. His fate as a respected scientist was uncertain.

mented, where they lived for two more months after their death sentence.

I have waited at the heavy iron doors before all of these prisons when in the last years I was in Berlin and had something "official" to do there. There I accompanied Aunt Ursel and Aunt Christel, Aunt Emmi and Maria, who often went there daily to bring or to pick up things. Often they came in vain; often they had to take the abuse of mean commissars. But sometimes they also found a friendly gate-keeper who thought like a human being and delivered a message, who accepted something outside the specified time or gave food to the prisoners in spite of the prohibition.

Yes, bringing food! It was not easy in the last years, and Aunt Ursel especially couldn't do enough in this regard. In the process, she starved herself until she was just a skeleton. There were tragedies, when Uncle Rüdiger sent the food back out again with the message that he had enough. Who believed that of him? Aunt Ursel sent it back in and it came back out again. Uncle Klaus, on the other hand, was different! He always consumed everything that was sent to him. Uncle Dietrich did not have it so bad as long as he sat in Tegel. He was on good terms with the prison personnel there, and the prison commandant was humane. Uncle Hans too did not at first have it bad. His prison com-mandant behaved in an almost friendly way toward him. But then he became sick, came into the Charité in the Surgical Clinic at Sauerbruch, where I saw him for the last time. After he had been brought into the prison again, he got scarlet fever and diphtheria and then lay in bed with severe postdiphtherial paralysis for almost half a year, eventually at the concentration camp at Oranienburg and in the State Hospital in Berlin.

And now! The last time I was in Berlin was at the end of March; I had to go back shortly before Grandpapa's seventy-seventh birthday. Uncle Klaus and Uncle Rüdiger were still alive then; Uncle Hans sent through his doctor news that was not completely devoid of hope; of Uncle Dietrich, who had been carried away from Berlin early in Febru-ary by the SS, there was no trace. It must have been on 8 April, shortly before my departure for Friedrichsbrunn to be with you, that I last telephoned your grandparents from Leipzig. At that time everything was still unchanged. That's now more than two months ago. What all may still have happened before the Russians captured the city? A man came from there and said that four thousand more political prisoners had been killed before that. And what might have happened during the capture and afterwards? Are all of them still alive? Will your grandparents still have been able to withstand these difficult days? Both were already at the limit of their strength. In the last years, Grandmama frequently had fainting spells with loss of memory, a result of the overexertion, agitation, and malnutrition of the last few years. They do not have any competent help in the house. Uncle Dietrich spoke to someone in detail as late as 5 April in the area around Passau.[2] From there he was to be brought to the Flossenbürg concentration camp near Weiden.

Why isn't he here yet? . . .

Karl Bonhoeffer to Professor Jossmann in Boston

Berlin
8 October 1945

. . . That we have experienced much evil and have lost two sons and two sons-in-law through the Gestapo, you have, as I hear, already learned. You can imagine that this has not passed by us old people without leaving its mark. Throughout the years, we stood under the pressure of concern for those imprisoned and those not yet imprisoned but endangered. But since all of us were agreed about the necessity of acting, and my sons also were aware of what awaited them in case the plot was unsuccessful, and had made their peace with life, we are certainly sad but also proud of their clear-cut behavior. We have beautiful memories of both sons from prison . . . that touch us and their friends very deeply. . . .

2. That was the day in Regensburg.

Regarding the Texts

The letters from Klaus Bonhoeffer to Cornelie (pp. 39–40), to his parents (pp. 40–42), and to his children (pp. 42–45) were published for the first time in Dietrich and Klaus Bonhoeffer, *Auf dem Wege zur Freiheit: Gedichte und Briefe aus der Haft*, 2d ed., ed. Eberhard Bethge (Berlin: Verlag Haus und Schule, 1947).

A letter from Christine von Dohnanyi to Ricarda Huch, from Munich on 12 November 1946, is the basic source for the information regarding Hans von Dohnanyi.

Parts of the letters of Hans von Dohnanyi from 25 February and 8 March 1945 have been cited before in Eberhard Bethge, *Dietrich Bonhoeffer: Theologe, Christ, Zeitgenosse*, 5th ed. (Munich: Christian Kaiser Verlag, 1983), 1020ff.

For the information regarding Justus Delbrück, the text by Annedore Leber from her *Das Gewissen entscheidet: Bereiche des deutschen Widerstandes von 1933–1945* (Berlin: Mosaik-Verlag, 1957), 284–86, was used.

The source for the information regarding Dietrich Bonhoeffer is a letter from Sabine Leibholz to Ricarda Huch, from Oxford on 14 November 1946. Added to this is the (somewhat shortened) contribution "Begegnungen in Tegel," by Susanne Dress, from Wolf-Dieter Zimmermann, ed., *Begegnungen mit Dietrich Bonhoeffer*, 4th ed. (Munich: Christian Kaiser Verlag, 1969), 188–94.

The letters of Dietrich Bonhoeffer printed here come from his *Widerstand und Ergebung: Briefe und Aufzeichnungen aus der Haft*, 2d ed., ed. Eberhard Bethge (Munich: Christian Kaiser Verlag, 1977), 401–4 and 434–37.

The letters from Karl Friedrich and Karl Bonhoeffer (pp. 113–15) have been quoted previously in Eberhard Bethge's Bonhoeffer biography cited above, 1042ff.

Regarding the Portraits

The pictures of Rüdiger Schleicher and Dietrich Bonhoeffer were made available by Eberhard and Renate Bethge. For the reproduction of the self-portrait of Hans von Dohnanyi, a sketch in pencil that originated in prison, we are indebted to Frau Barbara Bayer-von Dohnanyi. The picture of Klaus Bonhoeffer is the property of Frau Emmi Bonhoeffer. For the photograph of Justus Delbrück, we are indebted to Mr. Klaus Delbrück.